GOING VIRTUAL

GOING VIRTUAL

Programs and Insights from a Time of Crisis

SARAH OSTMAN

ALA Public Programs Office

ALA
Editions
CHICAGO | 2021

SARAH OSTMAN is the communications manager in the American Library Association's Public Programs Office, where she serves as editor of ProgrammingLibrarian.org, a web resource for library professionals. Before joining ALA and the library field in 2014, she spent nearly a decade as a newspaper reporter, editor, and freelance writer. She is the co-author of *Book Club Reboot: 71 Creative Twists* (ALA Editions, 2019) and co-editor of *Act, Listen, Empower: Grounding Your Library Work in Community Engagement* (ALA Editions, 2020). Ostman has an MA in journalism from Columbia College in Chicago and a BA in sociology and theater from Smith College in Massachusetts.

© 2021 by the American Library Association

Extensive effort has gone into ensuring the reliability of the information in this book; however, the publisher makes no warranty, express or implied, with respect to the material contained herein.

ISBNs
978-0-8389-4878-1 (paper)
978-0-8389-4880-4 (PDF)
978-0-8389-4943-6 (ePub)

Library of Congress Cataloging-in-Publication Data
Names: Ostman, Sarah, author.
Title: Going virtual : programs and insights from a time of crisis / Sarah Ostman.
Description: Chicago : ALA Editions, 2021. | "ALA Public Programs Office." | Includes bibliographical references and index. | Summary: "This book explores virtual programs created by library workers during the pandemic and also shares a handful of analog programs developed to serve communities using deliveries, take-home kits, window displays, and socially distanced interactions"—Provided by publisher.
Identifiers: LCCN 2020054843 (print) | LCCN 2020054844 (ebook) | ISBN 9780838948781 (paperback) | ISBN 9780838948804 (pdf) | ISBN 9780838949436 (epub)
Subjects: LCSH: Shared virtual environments—Library applications—United States—Case studies. | Libraries—Activity programs—United States—Case studies. | Libraries and community—United States—Case studies. | Libraries and public health—United States—Case studies. | COVID-19 Pandemic, 2020—United States—Case studies.
Classification: LCC Z678.93.S53 O85 2021 (print) | LCC Z678.93.S53 (ebook) | DDC 025.5—dc23
LC record available at https://lccn.loc.gov/2020054843
LC ebook record available at https://lccn.loc.gov/2020054844

Book design by Alejandra Diaz in the Chaparral Pro, Korolev, and Eurostile typefaces.

♾ This paper meets the requirements of ANSI/NISO Z39.48-1992 (Permanence of Paper).

Printed in the United States of America
25 24 23 22 21   5 4 3 2 1

For COLESON, JONAH, and THEO

CONTENTS

ACKNOWLEDGMENTS

Thanks to my colleagues in the ALA Public Programs Office: our fearless leader Deb Robertson, my wonderful supervisor Mary Davis Fournier, my dedicated colleagues BeeBee Browne, Lainie Castle, Samantha Oakley, Brian Russell, Melanie Welch, and especially Hannah Arata, who joined our team as communications associate in the midst of the pandemic and—though we have never worked in the same building—has quickly become a terrific partner.

Special thanks to my ALA colleagues Carrie Russell, Donna Seaman, Kristin Lahurd, Gwendolyn Prellwitz, and Amber Hayes, and to Courtney Breese of the National Coalition for Dialogue and Deliberation for sharing their expertise.

And of course, thank you to the following library workers for being so willing to share their programs and experiences with me. You have truly been pioneers through this difficult year.

Paul Addis, Coos Bay Public Library, Coos Bay, Oregon

Sadia Ahmed, Gail Borden Public Library, Elgin, Illinois

Jill Anderson, Queens Public Library, Queens, New York

Lauren Antolino, Cranford Public Library, Cranford, New Jersey

Carrie S. Banks, Brooklyn Public Library, Brooklyn, New York

Lena Gonzalez Berrios, Montclair Community Library, Prince William Public Library System, Dumfries, Virginia

Gee Bolland, Western Allegheny Community Library, Pittsburgh, Pennsylvania

Jen Bonnet, Raymond H. Fogler Library, University of Maine, Orono, Maine

Cara Brancoli, St. Ignatius College Prep, San Francisco, California

Jennifer Brewer, Jackson-Madison County Library, Jackson, Tennessee

Jennifer Brooks, Woodstock Public Library, Woodstock, Georgia

Kate-Lynn Brown, Piscataway Public Library, Piscataway, New Jersey

Ramona Burkey, Russell Library, Middletown, Connecticut

D. Scott Campbell, Plaistow Public Library, Plaistow, New Hampshire

Rebecca Campbell, Tavares Public Library, Tavares, Florida

Tayla Cardillo, Oak Lawn Branch Library, Cranston Public Library, Cranston, Rhode Island

Michelle Carter, Aram Public Library, Delavan, Wisconsin

Rachel Chapman, Westinghouse Campus Library, Brooklyn, New York

Melanie Taylor Coombs, McArthur Public Library, Biddeford, Maine

Lisa Detweiler, Garfield County Public Library District, Rifle, Colorado

Corey Farrenkopf, Sturgis Library, Barnstable, Massachusetts

Giovanna Fiorino-Iannace, Harrison Public Library, Harrison, New York

Jessica Frazier, Bloomingdale Public Library, Bloomingdale, Illinois

Lynn Gardner, Southington Public Library, Southington, Connecticut

Laura Gardoski, Abington Community Library, Clarks Summit, Pennsylvania

Carri Genovese, Indianapolis Public Library, Indianapolis, Indiana

Carlo Ghilli, Public Library of Empoli, Tuscany, Italy

Ian Gosse, Oak Park Public Library, Oak Park, Illinois

Diana Graham, Marshes of Glynn Libraries, Brunswick, Georgia

Renee Haines, Allentown Public Library, Allentown, Pennsylvania

Danielle Henson, Gail Borden Public Library District, Elgin, Illinois

Janie Hermann, Princeton Public Library, Princeton, New Jersey

Jessica Hilburn, Benson Memorial Library, Titusville, Pennsylvania

Jana Hill, Fort Worth Public Library, Fort Worth, Texas

Remington Hill, Mercer County District Library, Celina, Ohio

Leah Holloway, Augusta-Richmond County Public Library, Augusta, Georgia

Holly Howard, Bath County Memorial Library, Owingsville, Kentucky

Liz Hughes, Half Hollow Hills Community Library, Dix Hills, New York

Sandi Imperio, Santa Cruz Public Libraries, Aptos, California

Holly Jin, Skokie Public Library, Skokie, Illinois

Ashley Johnson, Vernon Area Public Library, Lincolnshire, Illinois

Christine M. Johnson, Attleboro Public Library, Attleboro, Massachusetts

Karmen Kelly, McMillan Memorial Library, Wisconsin Rapids, Wisconsin

Alice Knapp, The Ferguson Library, Stamford, Connecticut

Noelle Kozak, Pittston Memorial Library, Pittston, Pennsylvania

Erica Krivopal, Piscataway Public Library, Piscataway, New Jersey

Jeffrey Lambert, Queens Public Library, New York, New York

Liz Laribee, Arlington Public Library, Arlington, Virginia

Jennifer Leavitt, Snake River School/Community Library, Blackfoot, Idaho

Colleen Leddy, Stair District Library, Morenci, Michigan

Serianna Leyland, San Anselmo Public Library, San Anselmo, California

Emily Mazzoni, Monroe Township Library, Monroe Township, New Jersey

Christina McPhail, La Grange Park Public Library, La Grange Park, Illinois

Terry McQuown, Massachusetts Library System, Marlborough, Massachusetts

MJ Medel, formerly of Silver City Public Library, Silver City, New Mexico

Ruth Monnier, Leonard H. Axe Library, Pittsburg State University, Pittsburg, Kansas

Tara Montoney, Seneca Falls Library, Seneca Falls, New York

Abby Morrow, Ellsworth Public Library, Ellsworth, Maine

Gillian Murphy, Julia L. Butterfield Memorial Library, Cold Spring, New York

Chris Myers, Lake Oswego Public Library, Lake Oswego, Oregon

Daniel Page, Germantown Community Library, Germantown, Tennessee

Chelsea Paige, Nesmith Library, Windham, New Hampshire

Holly Parker, Vestavia Hills Library in the Forest, Vestavia Hills, Alabama

Joan Peiffer, Grove Family Library, Chambersburg, Pennsylvania

Joanne Percy, Liberty Lake Municipal Library, Liberty Lake, Washington

Sherry Beth Preston, Gering Public Library, Gering, Nebraska

Stephanie Race, University of North Florida Thomas G. Carpenter Library, Jacksonville, Florida

Lisa Rand, Boyertown Community Library, Boyertown, Pennsylvania

T. J. Rankin, Tyler Public Library, Tyler, Texas

Mary Beth Riedner, Creator, Tales & Travel

Angela Rines, Easton Area Public Library, Easton, Pennsylvania

Michael Robin, Katonah Village Library, Katonah, New York

Joy Robinson, Piscataway Public Library, Piscataway, New Jersey

Juan Rubio, Seattle Public Library, Seattle, Washington

Basya Samuels, Los Angeles Public Library, North Hollywood Amelia Earhart Regional Branch, Los Angeles, California

Nora Sanchez, Oak Park Public Library, Oak Park, Illinois

Catherine Schaeffer, King County Library System, King County, Washington

Evelyn Shapiro, Champaign Public Library, Champaign, Illinois

Laura Skalitzky, Princeton Public Library, Princeton, Wisconsin

Marianne Stoess, Kentucky Humanities, Lexington, Kentucky

Dorothy Stoltz, Carroll County Public Library, New Windsor, Maryland

Colette Strassburg, New Hanover County Public Library, Wilmington, North Carolina

Celina Tirona, Daly City Public Library, Daly City, California

Ashleigh Torres, El Dorado County Library, Placerville, California

Jillian Wagner, Newport News Public Library, Newport News, Virginia

Carrie Weaver, Peters Township Public Library, McMurray, Pennsylvania

Erin Weaver, Bridgeville Public Library/South Fayette Township Library, Bridgeville and Morgan, Pennsylvania

Charlie Westerink, Nederland Community Library, Nederland, Colorado

Amanda Westfall, Emmet O'Neal Library, Mountain Brook, Alabama

Heather Wicke, Brandywine Community Library, Topton, Pennsylvania

Jana Wiersma, Carson City Library, Carson City, Nevada

Bobbie Wrinkle, McCracken County Public Library, Paducah, Kentucky

Jennifer Zappulla, Cora J. Belden Library, Rocky Hill, Connecticut

Rachel Zukowski, Prince George's County Memorial Library System, Prince George's County, Maryland

INTRODUCTION

arch 12, 2020, was a normal day, more or less. At ALA's headquarters in downtown Chicago, we were mask-free, at our desks, perhaps a little distracted by the news of this tiny virus that had been sweeping the world.

That day, a Thursday, was the first time I heard the phrase *social distancing*. It came from Jeffrey Lambert, assistant director of digital inclusion and workforce readiness at Queens Public Library and then chair of ALA's Public and Cultural Programs Advisory Committee. "We want to be reactive in a way that's science-informed," he said, "and since we are not the experts on pandemics, we are pulling in the experts wherever we can."

I had been learning a lot on the subject. Earlier I had e-mailed with an Italian librarian, Carlo Ghilli, head of cultural heritage library services at the Public Library of Empoli. He told me that shops, bars, and all of Tuscany were shuttered; Italian libraries, his included, had been closed for a week. Carlo sent me surreal pictures of an empty reading room and said his colleagues were offering storytelling by telephone and inviting famous Italian children's book writers to make video storytimes for Facebook. "Early in the outbreak we thought we could keep the library open by placing limits on how many people could enter at once," he said, "but we were eventually forced to close completely."

It all seemed unthinkable. Shops, bars, libraries—all of society—shutting down? How would we in the United States manage? What would we do?

We found out soon enough, with U.S. libraries following in Italian libraries' footsteps in the days and weeks that followed. The shutdown happened in waves. First, library workers dragged chairs into storage rooms to force visitors to socially distance, powered down half or two-thirds of their computers and taped "do not use" signs to those monitors, and removed toys from children's play areas. Then, programs were canceled and meeting rooms cordoned off. Eventually bold announcements started appearing on library home pages: "closed until further notice." The closures were as widespread as they felt; 99 percent of libraries responding to an ALA poll—that included more than 3,800 public, school, college and university, and other library types in all 50 states—reported limiting access to their buildings.[1]

It was scary and overwhelming, but at the same time a "we're all in this together" ethos took hold across the profession. Librarian listservs and Facebook groups flooded with people—library workers, of course, but also teachers, authors, and others—sharing resources and ideas to educate, prepare, and empower communities. Programming librarians moved their efforts online, posting storytimes (and debating fair use exceptions—see the fair use text box in chapter 1) and amping up the use of their social media pages. Again, the data showed that the surge of online activity was immediate; 61 percent of public libraries reported expanding virtual programming in a March 2020 Public Library Association study, just days and weeks after COVID-19 closed their doors.[2]

Of course, the pandemic wasn't the only thing on people's minds. Protests and civil unrest over police brutality and racism, record unemployment, and raging wildfires all combined into what *Rolling Stone* called "2020: The Year of the Converging Crises."[3]

In ALA's Public Programs Office, we believe that good library programming makes communities stronger and more resilient by creating lifelong learners, fostering conversation, and forging connections. These things—for simplicity's sake, we can boil them down to learning and talking—are especially important in the polarized political climate we live in, and exponentially more so during this national health crisis. To put it lightly, the challenge for libraries in 2020 was how to create good programming when it seemed impossible for people to make connections.

Spoiler alert: libraries did create good programming, even great programming. And they did it by thinking locally and being there for their communities, whether face-to-face or through a screen, one person at a time.

This is where this book picks up—with the creative, diverse, and thoughtful work that programming librarians did during the pandemic. In the following pages, we explore 90 programs and hear from the library workers who created them. Most of the programs we talk about were virtual, hosted online via a videoconferencing platform, or posted to social media. But we also look at a handful of analog programs that were developed to serve communities using deliveries, take-home kits, window displays, and socially distanced interactions. I learned about these achievements in various ways—through individual videoconferences with library workers, e-mail exchanges, submissions to Programming Librarian, a website I run in ALA's Public Programs Office, and responses to an online survey looking for notable virtual programs. I quote from these conversations and submissions throughout this book.

 Be on the lookout for this icon to find the analog programs discussed throughout this book.

Let's not sugarcoat it: in most cases, these changes have been neither easy nor fun. On May 12, Chelsea Price, director of the Meservey Public Library in Iowa, wrote about her anxiety in re-opening her library for Programming Librarian. "I'm willing to bet your education and training did not prepare you for this," she wrote, adding, "the world is a Dumpster fire, and we are all just doing the best we can."[4]

Even the technology has added a new burden. "It's been exhausting, in many ways, to do this," Janie Hermann, manager of adult programming at the Princeton Public Library in New Jersey, told me in October. "Every Crowdcast you do, you have to be prepared for things to go wrong with the tech at any time," she says. "And then you have to be calm under pressure." (Crowdcast is a live video platform preferred by many libraries and publishers, especially for large events.)

And we need to acknowledge right off the bat the inherent inequities of library's virtual shift. The digital divide is real, and we see it. The fact that millions of Americans cannot access vital information when they need it most, like during COVID-19, is a massive concern and will no doubt be the subject of many books.

But a lot of heartwarming things happened, too. Here are just a few that I came across while writing this book:

- During the shutdown in Morenci, Michigan, people howled at the moon together from their homes on Facebook Live.
- Eighty library patrons in Lincolnshire, Illinois, toasted each other in a virtual beer tasting.
- A librarian in Nederland, Colorado, said he was hungry in a storytime so a patron brought him a sandwich.[5]

I hope you find inspiration in these pages. As always, my colleagues and I in the ALA Public Programs Office welcome your feedback; we invite you to reach out to tell us about programs that have been meaningful in your community. We can be reached at publicprograms@ala.org.

NOTES

1. "Public Libraries Respond to COVID-19: Survey of Response & Activities (May 2020)," Public Library Association, May 2020, www.ala.org/pla/issues/covid-19/surveyoverview.
2. "Public Libraries Respond to COVID-19: Survey of Response & Activities (March 2020)," Public Library Association, March 2020, www.ala.org/pla/issues/covid-19/march2020survey.
3. Mary Annaïse Heglar, "2020: The Year of the Converging Crises," *Rolling Stone*, October 4, 2020, www.rollingstone.com/politics/political-commentary/2020-crises-wildfires-pandemic-election-climate-crisis-1069907/.
4. Chelsea Price, "What Now?! Thoughts on Re-opening My Library in a Pandemic," Programming Librarian, May 12, 2020, https://programminglibrarian.org/blog/what-now-thoughts-re-opening-my-library-pandemic.
5. Colleen Leddy (library director, Stair District Library, Morenci, Michigan), e-mail message to author, November 1, 2020; Ashley Johnson, "Program Model: Virtual Beer Tasting," Programming Librarian, May 7, 2020, https://programminglibrarian.org/programs/virtual-beer-tasting; Charlie Westerink (library assistant, Nederland [CO] Community Library), e-mail message to author, October 31, 2020.

ABOUT THIS BOOK

The structure of this book is based on the mission statement of the ALA Public Programs Office: "to empower libraries to create vibrant hubs of learning, conversation and connection in communities of all types." I start by talking about library programs whose primary goal are *Learning*; then ones that spark *Conversation*; then those that create *Connection* in a time when connection can seem challenging, rare, and much needed.

Finally, I add a fourth category not explicitly stated in our Public Programs Office mission statement—programs meant mainly to *Entertain*—because I think we can all agree that laughter is pretty critical to wellbeing; it was especially critical in 2020 and libraries knew it. Admittedly, these categories get blurry, and most programs in this book can easily fit into two or three of them.

How did I land on this precise list of programs, you may be wondering? In June 2020, I posted a survey to Programming Librarian calling for submissions. "With COVID-19, many libraries were thrown into uncharted terrain when it came to programming," the call-for-submission said. "And so—as libraries do—they quickly innovated, coming up with a vast array of virtual programs in a short time. Some were twists on old favorites while others were brand new concepts." The survey was shared via social media, electronic mailing lists, e-newsletters, and word of mouth. More than 700 library workers submitted programs for consideration. I supplemented these submissions with unique programs that I heard about through contacts in the library field, colleagues, the Programming Librarian Facebook group, and article submissions to Programming Librarian.

In addition to the programs in this book, I cover best practices on various topics and indulge in Q&As with leaders from the field on topics such as measuring program impact, understanding copyright law, moderating virtual author talks, facilitating virtual conversations, and injecting personality into your social media presence.

CHAPTER ONE

LEARNING

I n this section, we look at educational programs—teaching everything from fake news to fitness, wildflowers to witchcraft. Throughout the pandemic, libraries have persevered in their mission to create lifelong learners.

ART TALK TUESDAYS

San Anselmo Public Library
San Anselmo, California

San Anselmo Public Library's Art Talk Tuesday is a one-hour, docent-led program featuring popular exhibits currently or formerly on display at local museums, including the de Young Museum, Legion of Honor, and Asian Art Museum of San Francisco. Typically, the talk is held in Town Hall Council Chambers, but the pandemic brought the series online. In May 2020, a docent from the San Francisco Museum of Modern Art presented on San Francisco art from the '50s to the '70s; in September, the series covered three California master painters. Other presentations have included "The Language of Flowers in Japanese Art" with the Asian Art Museum and "Last Supper in Pompeii" with the Fine Arts Museums of San Francisco. The recordings are archived on the library's YouTube page.

BILINGUAL KWENTUHAN

Daly City Public Library
Daly City, California

Daly City, with a population of 106,000, is the largest city with a majority Asian population in the mainland United States. Fifty-seven percent of its residents identify as Asian American, and more than one-third of the total population is Filipino. Celina Tirona, library assistant and a person of Filipino heritage, called her program Bilingual Kwentuhan, using the Tagalog word for storytime. "It was so nice to share our first storytime for the Filipino community," Tirona said. "The program has received more views than any of our other virtual programs, and the publisher is sending us books and bookmarks as thanks for the exposure." Tirona pre-recorded the first *Kwentuhan* in June 2020 and posted it as a Facebook Premiere at the time of the event. Participants could watch and listen to Tagalog children's songs and a reading of a Tagalog children's book with its translation. Twenty people tuned in live that first time, and the recording has more than 8,000 views—making it the library's most viewed virtual program. It is so popular that the library has continued to offer the program biweekly.

COMMUNITY COOKING WITH THE CO-OP: STARRING JAMAR

Coos Bay Public Library
Coos Bay, Oregon

Coos Bay Public Library partnered with the outreach coordinator at Coos Head Food Co-op for a live cooking demo. People joined Jamar Ruff and reference librarian Paul Addis on Zoom while Ruff made chana aloo curry (chickpea curry with potato) from the co-op kitchen. When people registered, they received the Zoom link as well as a list of ingredients, so many attendees followed along in their own kitchens with their cameras running. While Ruff cooked and provided instructions, viewers commented in the chat box and Addis read the comments aloud. Ruff also used some solid cooking-show techniques, such as bringing items closer to the camera so viewers could see ingredients up close. "I had never done a program like this virtually, so my main challenge was preparing for the unknown . . . it was a little overwhelming managing everything by myself," Addis said. "But my community partner's smile when all the participants left Zoom . . . that moment was priceless and made it all worthwhile." The collaboration resulted in a new partnership, with monthly programs on the fourth Thursday of each month.

COOKING MATTERS POP-UP GROCERY STORE TOUR: ONLINE

Ellsworth Public Library
Ellsworth, Maine

Ellsworth Public Library partnered with a local community health nonprofit to present an online grocery store tour and to share tips about shopping healthy on a budget. Featuring a Maine SNAP-Ed nutrition educator, the one-hour presentation covered how to use the U.S. Department of Agriculture's MyPlate app as a shopping guide, buy fruit and vegetables on a budget, compare unit pricing, and read nutrition labels. The presenters started the hour by inviting participants to write in the chat to introduce themselves and share why they had signed up for the program. "This accomplished two goals—by learning why they signed up for the program, [the presenter] was able to tailor the information to fit their interests, and it was also a good check to make sure that everyone knew how to access and use the chat," said community engagement librarian Abby Morrow.

COVID-19 MISINFORMATION CHALLENGE

Raymond H. Fogler Library, University of Maine
Orono, Maine

Does the World Health Organization recommend injecting disinfectant to treat COVID-19? Can the virus flourish in rolls of toilet paper? In the early days of the pandemic, the internet was rife with misinformation. The University of Maine's Raymond H. Fogler Library used it as an opportunity to teach people around the world to discern fact from fiction. For five days in May 2020, people who registered received an e-mail quiz designed to test their knowledge while having fun and learning something new. The Google Form quizzes asked people to evaluate the validity of memes, doctors, news headlines, treatments, and some of the science behind the virus. After completing the quiz, individuals received scores and links to resources. More than 500 people signed up for the e-mails, including university faculty, staff, and students, as well as librarians, parents, and others from across the United States, Canada, Hungary, the Netherlands, Jordan, and China. "We received myriad, unsolicited responses from enthusiastic participants who wanted to share their experience with each day's challenge," said social sciences and humanities librarian Jen Bonnet. "We heard from parents taking the challenge with children, partners and spouses comparing notes and scores, and teachers sharing the challenge with their students. Some even said they didn't want the challenge to end."

If you want to take or view the quizzes, they are available from the library's LibGuide (https://libguides.library.umaine.edu/covid19).

CREATIVITY CRATES FOR SUMMER READING

Bath County Memorial Library
Owingsville, Kentucky

Holly Howard, the assistant director of outreach and programming at Bath County Memorial Library, calls the Reading Creativity Crate program "the socially distanced solution to our summer reading program." "Many of our patrons love and rely on summer reading so we knew we had to make it work," Howard says. Library staff created five age-level crates for patrons to choose from: pre-K, grades 1–4, grades 5–8, grades 9–12, and adult. Staff started by sharing test crates with some of their own children. "The kids told us what they liked and didn't like about the crates, including their thoughts on the overall presentation," Howard says. The final crates each included two books, supplies for two crafts, supplemental resources for additional crafts, and a brochure recommending similar books. Patrons could pick up new boxes every two weeks or library staff would deliver them to homes.

CRICUT STICKER MAKING

Monroe Township Library
Monroe Township, New Jersey

When teen services librarian Emily Mazzoni's library closed to the public, it seemed a shame to let their $350 Cricut Maker sit unused in the library makerspace. So with her director's permission, she brought the printer-sized cutting machine home for a virtual program with a mail component. Mazzoni used screen share to demonstrate the Design Space app, where teens learned how to create vinyl stickers. Mazzoni then printed them out while the teens watched. "There was an added element of fun because while I peeled back the stickers, they guessed which one was which," she said. Mazzoni mailed the stickers to the teens' homes. "They loved that because they don't really get fun physical mail," she said. Mazzoni later offered a similar program using iron-on transfers, where she showed the teens how to iron on the decals once they arrived in the mail.

DREAM CAREERS: VIRUS HUNTERS

King County Library System
King County, Washington

Dream Careers is a teen-initiated, teen-led series designed to increase awareness on a variety of career choices. The program helps teens research career paths while speaking with a chosen guest. The kickoff event featured virologist Dr. Ken Stedman, a professor in Portland State University's biology department. Dr. Stedman studies viruses found in extreme environments, such as in volcanic hot springs, and the teens wanted to hear from him in light of the pandemic. The teens decided to structure the program like an informational interview and planned the questions in advance. "Our teen volunteers took turns asking Dr. Stedman questions, and we had time for other participants to ask questions on camera and in the chat box," said teen services librarian Catherine Schaeffer. Topics included the typical workday of a virologist, the equipment he uses, and the protective gear he wears while in the lab.

Marketing Virtual Programs

When Marianne Stoess's organization first moved its programming online in response to the pandemic, she was inspired by the possibilities: "Literally the whole world is your audience. Anybody could come," says Stoess, assistant director of marketing and public relations for Kentucky Humanities.

Over time, she saw how this could also be a drawback: your audience could also *attend* programs literally anywhere. "Before, we were competing with events in our city on that day," Stoess says. "The whole world is our competition now."

With so many virtual events available, marketing your library's programs can feel like a daunting task, but it doesn't have to be. If you aren't getting the turnout you want, try following these six tips:

1. **Clearly specify when events are virtual.** It might be obvious to you whether a program is in-person or virtual, but that's not always the case for people who come across your website or click through one of your newsletter links. Make sure the distinction is clear. "Our website still uses the same event calendar for virtual programs, but I started adding a 'Virtual' marker at the start of each title to make it clear we were not meeting in person," says Chelsea Paige, social media/emerging technology librarian at the Nesmith Library in New Hampshire.

2. **Don't underestimate word of mouth.** With so many online events to choose from, people are going to be drawn to those that are recommended by people they trust. Ask your Friends groups, trustees, or regulars to spread the word. As Stoess suggests, "people who are feeling virtual fatigue might be more inclined to log in to an event if they hear it directly from a friend."

3. **Partner.** It is not cheating to share the program workload with another library or organization. In *Ask, Listen, Empower: Grounding Your Library Work in Community Engagement*, Cindy Fesemyer explains "you need to know yourself to know what kind of partner you need. Looking at the things you do well is a good start."[m] If your library's strength is not marketing, look to partner with groups that have strong followings, and you can bring your other strengths (whether that be technology, staff, or something else) to the table.

4. **Ask people what they want.** A Google Form or SurveyMonkey questionnaire—the shorter, the better—can be a quick way to gauge interest or poll your community to find out if you're hitting your marks. "We surveyed our adult patrons to learn what type of virtual programming they would watch on social media," says

Carrie Weaver, public relations coordinator at Peters Township Public Library in Pennsylvania. "We sent out a one-question, multiple-choice survey and received 725 responses. That proved to be an excellent guide for our limited library staff working from home!"

5. **Seize the moment.** Have you noticed there's a lot going on these days? Your marketing, as well as your programs, should show that your library is active in your community and that you have skin in the game. Angela Rines, marketing and public relations manager at the Easton Area Public Library in Pennsylvania, says her library has been focusing on a greater commitment to antiracism. "This really has been an opportunity to seize the moment and try new things when it comes to building a virtual community and marketing virtual programs," she says.

6. **Fail forward.** Marketing these days—heck, *most things* these days—is challenging. There is no rule book; sometimes the best we can do is be willing to try new things and pay attention to what works. "Planning virtual events in the pandemic has proven to be a mad dash instead of a long campaign because things are changing so rapidly," Stoess says. "The world will probably be a pretty different place in a week or two!"

EXTREME IN THE MAINSTREAM

Gail Borden Public Library
Elgin, Illinois

Extremist groups—the Proud Boys, Boogaloo, and the Base—that used to lurk in the shadows are now in the news and in the public eye. Where did these groups come from? What drives their actions and ideologies? What potential impact do they have on our community? In November 2020, Gail Borden Public Library hosted a panel discussion featuring experts on extremism to explore these questions. The panel included Dr. Elizabeth Yates, senior researcher at the National Consortium for the Study of Terrorism and Responses to Terrorism at the University of Maryland; David Goldenberg, Midwest regional director of the Anti-Defamation League; a local city council member; and a rabbi. The conversation was moderated by a local attorney.

The decision to host the program was made in response to the first presidential debate in September, during which President Donald Trump addressed a far-right extremist group, saying "Proud Boys, stand back and stand by."[2]

FAKE NEWS AND CORONAVIRUS: WHAT YOU NEED TO KNOW TO STAY SAFE

Plaistow Public Library
Plaistow, New Hampshire

In the early days of the pandemic, Plaistow Public Library set out to debunk some of the misinformation that was running rampant on social media. Residents of Plaistow, a small town of 8,000 located about 40 miles north of Boston, had questions: Was COVID-19 developed in a lab? Can dogs spread the disease? Does 5G have anything to do with it? The library invited Randall Mikkelson, a managing editor at Thomson Reuters, former White House reporter, and Plaistow resident, to share tips that could help people separate fact from fiction and stop the spread of misinformation. The program was structured as a one-on-one, socially distanced conversation and was filmed at the library. The program aired on Facebook Live on both the library's account and the local public access TV livestream. "With our fabulous cable access guy running the videoboard, we were able to switch the video feed between us and the journalist's slide show seamlessly," said interviewer Scott Campbell, the library's assistant director and adult programming manager. "While we thought it was a super important topic, the people who most needed to watch and learn about the myths were those least likely to tune in. Ultimately this is why we chose to record the program and have it rebroadcast on local access television—hoping to expand the reach of the important messages in the program."

You can view the recording on Vimeo at https://vimeo.com/410440259.

FIT LIT BOOK DISCUSSION

Indianapolis Public Library
Indianapolis, Indiana

When COVID-19 struck, Indianapolis Public Library had plans in place for a walking book group: participants would read a book, meet at the library, and then discuss it while going on a walk together. With that plan suddenly unsafe, staff decided to shift the group online and created the Fit Lit Book Discussion, a collaboration with the Marion County Department of Health. In monthly Zoom meetings, participants discuss a book virtually, listen to a health expert, and encourage each other in healthy habits and physical activity. Book titles have included *The RBG Workout: How She Stays Strong . . . and You Can Too!* by Bryant Johnson and *The Body: A Guide for Occupants* by Bill Bryson. There is a corresponding private Facebook group, where members can continue their discussions after the meetings. "If I could give one piece of advice to anyone intimidated by creating a program from scratch, it would be to remember that experts at other community organizations are often available and excited to share their resources," says librarian Carri Genovese, who leads the group with her colleague Marianne Kruppa.

GARDENING IN SMALL PLACES

Sturgis Library
Barnstable, Massachusetts

If you were a city dweller or apartment renter during quarantine, chances are your world felt a bit smaller. In early May, Cape Cod's Sturgis Library offered a program to teach patrons how to create pollinator gardens and edible landscapes if they didn't have much space or own property. "We had been offering many native gardening programs focused on getting people to understand the benefits of healthy gardening, but this was the first we held directed at people who may not be able to garden in a traditional sense, such as apartment renters," says assistant director Corey Farrenkopf. "We want to make environmentalism accessible to all." The program was led by certified horticulturalist Cashel O'Sullivan and moderated by Farrenkopf over Zoom. Patrons watched a slide show and then discussed what would be best to plant in their small gardens. Thanks to a grant from the Vermont Community Foundation, the library mailed each participant a curated assortment of seeds, picked out by the horticulturist, to start their gardens. "People were very happy to receive seeds when it was difficult to go out in person to get them," Farrenkopf recalls.

THE HISTORY OF WITCHCRAFT

Champaign Public Library and the University of Illinois Rare Book and Manuscript Library
Champaign, Illinois

No one could have predicted that a virtual lecture on the history of witchcraft presented by a downstate public library and university rare book room would capture the attention of tens, if not hundreds, of thousands of people. But just before Halloween 2020, it did. "The Facebook event was shared by an antiquarian book collector group in Boston, other libraries, other rare book archives, academics—there's been more tagging than I've ever seen," said Evelyn Shapiro, promotions manager at the Champaign Public Library. "At one point I asked people where they were from and that returned an extraordinary list of places: Baku, Berlin, New Orleans, Mexico City, and on and on." The event featured Dr. Cait Coker and Ruthann Miller, curators of rare books and manuscripts who specialize in medieval and early modern literatures and cultures. Drawing on sixteenth- and seventeenth-century manuscripts, books, and herbals, they discussed the case of the Lancashire witches whose arrests, trials, and executions captured the attention of the day. The lecture was originally planned as a registration-required event on Zoom, but when demand went sky-high, organizers decided to livestream the event on YouTube and Facebook. Nearly 140,000 people marked themselves as "interested" on Facebook; 3,000 people tuned in for the live broadcast on October 29, and more than 10,000 people had viewed the YouTube video a day later.

KNITTING FOR KNEWBIES

Western Allegheny Community Library
Pittsburgh, Pennsylvania

Studies have shown that knitting, with its calming, repetitive motions, can have therapeutic effects. Knitting for Knewbies was a three-day Zoom camp where kids in grades two through six learned to knit during the pandemic. "I've been knitting since I was six years old," says early literacy outreach specialist Gee Bolland, who led the class. "It's such a good hobby for busy hands." The library spent about $150 to create and distribute kits containing yarn, needles, and patterns, that were available by curbside pickup, and together they covered eight different knitting skills—tying a slip knot, casting on, knitting, yarn overs, two different increases, and two different decreases— over three consecutive days. Bolland used two cameras, with one focused on her face and the other on her hands, which was helpful for walking through the various techniques. "One of the girls in the program took to knitting like a fish takes to water," Bolland recalls. "After our first day, she was in two other programs, one with my manager and another with myself, and she was knitting the whole time. It made me so happy to see her take to it so quickly."

LUNCH WITH THE LIBRARY: PREDATORY VS. PROFESSIONAL JOURNALS

University of North Florida Thomas G. Carpenter Library
Jacksonville, Florida

Predatory journals are exploitative academic journals that charge author fees without providing the editorial and peer-review processes that legitimate journals do—in essence, scamming academics and creating poor-quality publications. The University of North Florida (UNF) Thomas G. Carpenter Library hosted a virtual brown-bag lunch program to help faculty identify these fraudulent journals from reputable ones. Head of research and outreach Stephanie Race invited faculty to submit questions in advance and developed an accompanying LibGuide. The discussion, along with the rest of the Lunch with the Library series, was offered in collaboration with the UNF Office of Faculty Enhancement's virtual faculty lounge, an online resource on the university's Canvas platform. "As a result of each session in this series, faculty have made contact with the library for additional assistance," Race says. "It provides an opportunity to remind faculty that the library is still available to support them not only in their classroom instruction but also in their research and publishing."

MCLIB LIVE: FUNERALS AND GRIEF DURING COVID

McCracken County Public Library
Paducah, Kentucky

McCracken County Public Library hosted a series of guest speakers on topics of importance during the pandemic. Programs were offered on Zoom and averaged 45 minutes; after the live sessions, the recordings were uploaded to the library's YouTube page for later viewing. According to adult program coordinator Bobbie Wrinkle, one especially impactful topic was the session on grieving and funerals during COVID, which featured the director from a local funeral home. The director presented slides about how funerals have changed and adapted during the pandemic—from restrictions on funeral home staff hugging people or shaking hands to selling caskets online—and how families are coping. "In a normal scene at a funeral service, you will have a lot of visits at the funeral, not only immediate family but friends, coworkers . . . the families gain a lot of support," Wrinkle says. "That's been one of the hardest things we've seen for families is not having that support around them." Other presentations covered violence and COVID-19, featuring the director of a crisis center, and volunteering during a pandemic, with a representative of the local United Way.

MICROGREENS FOR BEGINNERS

Southington Public Library
Southington, Connecticut

Microgreens are the edible, nutrient-rich seedlings of vegetables, such as radishes, broccoli, cilantro, or basil, that can be added as garnishes to salads, soups, and other dishes. Southington Public Library partnered with the local

Gently Grown Farms for a Zoom primer on how to grow and consume the superfood at home without using expensive or complicated equipment. The plants can be grown year-round and in small spaces, making them a good fit for home quarantine gardeners who want to try something new.

PINK SUPERMOON VIEWING PARTY

Stair District Library
Morenci, Michigan

On April 7, library director Colleen Leddy and her husband took a drive to a little-traveled country road, where they hosted a nighttime watch party on Facebook Live for the rising of the Pink Supermoon. "We had a trivia contest while waiting for the moon to rise and gave away some goofy [prizes and] some good prizes, including then highly prized rolls of toilet paper," Leddy said. "As the moon rose, my husband, the president of the (fake) Morenci Howling Society, began howling at the moon, and those watching on Facebook from their homes were invited to join in." Supermoons occur when the moon is close to perigee—the closest that the moon gets to the Earth in its elliptic orbit—making it appear bigger and brighter than usual; as the first supermoon of the year, April's supermoon is nicknamed the Pink Supermoon. The moon doesn't actually appear pink; it's named after a wildflower that blooms in springtime. The event took place during Michigan's statewide lockdown.

SOCIALLY DISTANCED WILDFLOWER WALK

Gering Public Library
Gering, Nebraska

Public services librarian Sherry Beth Preston's last job involved plants, so she knows a lot about wildflowers. Over several weeks in June 2020, she created a "wildflower walk" in the Nebraska prairie to encourage patrons to get out and safely enjoy the outdoors. Preston spent an afternoon on a hillside with a plant book and marked 25 wildflowers with numbered flags. Next, she listed the plants with a few interesting facts about each and created a PDF file. She printed some copies to keep at the library and uploaded the file to the website along with a map of where to find the flagged plants. She also recommended wildflower books that were part of the library's collection as well as wildflower and bird identification apps. People learned about the wildflower walk via the library's website or Facebook page and could go out on their own to hike through the prairie and learn about the flowers. As the weeks went on, different plants bloomed so Preston added them to the plant line. Aside from an antelope that enjoyed snacking on the flags and flowers, the walk was well received and completed by at least 20 people. An unexpected bonus: "I got to use my Range Management degree in my library job!" Preston said.

SPARK JOY: ORGANIZE YOUR HOME

Harrison Public Library
Harrison, New York

There's nothing like a quarantine to make folks have a reckoning with their clutter. With people spending more time at home, the Harrison Public Library hosted an organization program with Karin Socci, a gold certified Marie Kondo consultant and founder of a home organization business, the Serene Home. During the program, Socci showed patrons how to tackle their closets and restore order to their homes and lives. "We knew many of our patrons were spending time at home and searching for productive projects," said adult programming and outreach librarian Giovanna Fiorino-Iannace. "It was good to have a program topic that everyone could relate to during quarantine."

STARTUP SHARP WITH THE AUGUSTA LIBRARY

Augusta-Richmond County Public Library
Augusta, Georgia

Knowing that many in their community had lost their source of income during the pandemic, Augusta-Richmond County Public Library sought to provide a free service that gave expert advice and resources to help people get through the difficult time. The result was Startup Sharp with the Augusta Library, a four-part webinar series that taught people how to begin their own small business from home. Library staff connected with professors from the James M. Hull College of Business at Augusta University as well as a marketing and communications specialist from the Georgia Cancer Center, who presented slides about business plans, marketing, and financing tools. The program was livestreamed on Facebook, Twitter, and YouTube weekly from July 20 to August 10.

STEAM-Y WONDERFUL WEDNESDAYS

Los Angeles Public Library, North Hollywood Amelia Earhart Regional Branch
Los Angeles, California

What happens when you pour milk onto a plate, add a few dots of food coloring, and plop a dish soap–covered cotton swab into the middle of it all? The answer has to do with hydrophilic and hydrophobic properties, and we won't spoil the surprise, but you can find out that and more on the North Hollywood Amelia Earhart Regional Library's Facebook and Instagram accounts. In the weekly video series STEAM-Y Wonderful Wednesdays, Los Angeles Public Library children's librarian Basya Samuels uses everyday household items to demonstrate fun science experiments. Early in the pandemic, Samuels started creating the videos in her home kitchen with her assistant/daughter Esther alongside her (and with another daughter manning the camera); since then, the team has covered bubbling blobs, spinning tornadoes, underwater volcanoes, and many more experiments. After each demo, Samuels explains the science behind the experiments in kid-friendly terms. "Sometimes explaining complicated science concepts trip me up, but my girls help me make it understandable for families," Samuels says. "Kids love trying new things, and science can be a lot of fun. Plus, it's educational, which makes parents happy too."

Measuring the Impact of Your Virtual Programs

Virtual programs, like in-person ones, can be evaluated with the goal of improving over time. In fact, virtual programming impact was an important measure of success during COVID-19 closures, especially when typical indicators of success, like gate counts and circulation figures, didn't tell the whole story.

But how do you gauge the success of your virtual programs? Attendance for a synchronous event? For a video or social media post, maybe it's the number of "likes" or "shares"? Janie Hermann, manager of adult programming at the Princeton Public Library in New Jersey, has years of experience assessing programs. Here are her ideas for taking a big-picture approach to understanding your programs' worth:

1. **Views are important, but maybe not how you think.** It's tempting to home in on social media counts because they provide hard data, but these numbers can provide a false narrative. "Your YouTube video could have 500 views, but how many people stayed for the whole thing?" Hermann says. "Were they really engaging, or did they say 'huh!' and keep scrolling?"

   To get a full picture, dig deeper into your social media analytics; most platforms offer information about engagement or average view duration. Understanding these analytics can help you create better content going forward, too. Princeton Public Library has learned that most people would only watch a storytime for seven or eight minutes, so they don't make them any longer than that.

2. **Comments matter, too.** Have you ever heard the saying "the plural of anecdote is data"?[3] Remember that the next time you receive an e-mail from a grateful patron. "If people spontaneously reach out to you, if even one person takes the time, that's meaningful," Hermann says. You can also download the comment section from events on many videoconferencing platforms. This is impact-measurement gold; share highlights with other staff, Friends groups, or trustees.

3. **For big events, send a survey.** Online surveys are simple to create, and if you collected registration, you should have e-mail addresses for attendees. Send them a few questions to get feedback via a free platform like SurveyMonkey or Google Forms, or use the Public Library Association's Project Outcome, an excellent (and free) surveying toolkit designed to help libraries measure and analyze outcomes. Another instant-gratification option: on some videoconferencing platforms, such as Zoom, you can enable a pop-up survey that appears on patrons' screens when the event ends.

4. **Build time into the process for reflection.** The goal of assessing programs is to improve, and that's only possible when you make it a priority. Plan a debriefing meeting after events, even if it's just a quick get-together in the virtual room after your attendees leave.

STEM CREATIVITY KITS

Stair District Library
Morenci, Michigan

When the governor's executive order closed her library in spring 2020, library director Colleen Leddy pivoted to distribute STEM (science, technology, learning, and math) kits through the local elementary school. Library and school staff worked together to assemble the take-home kits, which contained 21 budget-friendly items and instruction sheets to guide kids in completing ten different activities. It was important that the kits contained everything that was needed as Leddy knew some homes were struggling financially and would not have the materials on hand. Nearly 65 percent of students in the region receive free or reduced lunch. "While instruction sheets included links to websites, the goal of the kit was for students to explore the materials without needing to go online. In the library's rural area, there are still many families for whom internet access is not a given," Leddy says. Using the watercolor paint, crayons, Elmer's glue, pipe cleaners, poster board, and other materials from the kits, kids could build a catapult, a straw rocket, and a "sound sandwich," among other things. Some of the activities were drawn from NASA's Space Place, Steve Spangler Science, and the San Francisco Exploratorium. The project was part of a NASA @ My Library grant from ALA and the Space Science Institute's National Center for Interactive Learning.

THIS WEEK IN NEWPORT NEWS HISTORY

Newport News Public Library
Newport News, Virginia

Episode one of This Week in Newport News History starts with senior librarian Jillian Wagner pulling a genealogy file box off a shelf in the Newport News Public Library stacks. "The city's oldest tomb, a new city hall, and development in the Oyster Point area," she begins. "I'm Jillian Wagner, and welcome to This Week in Newport News History." Over the next three minutes, the viewer is taken to June 5, 1667, when Dutch warships fired on English ships off the coast of the then colony; the dedication of a new ten-story city hall building on June 4, 1972, an attempt to revitalize downtown; and June 5, 1986, a groundbreaking ceremony for an $18 million shopping mall built on a former dairy farm. The series, which began in June 2020, started as a way to keep people connected to library resources during the pandemic. "Libraries were closed," Wagner recalls. "Local museums were also closed. We felt that a weekly educational video series would give people access to historical content at a time when they could not research in person." The series is now being shown on the local public access television station as well as on the library's social media accounts.

VIRTUAL SIGN LANGUAGE

Brooklyn Public Library
Brooklyn, New York

"Due to our diverse city, we should learn to communicate with everyone," the Virtual Sign Language event description reads. Brooklyn Public Library's American Sign Language courses—first an in-person offering, moved online during the pandemic—are the result of a partnership with ADAPT Community Network, a New York City nonprofit for people with disabilities. The class is open to people of all ages and is ideal for first-time learners and those who want to strengthen their conversational skills. According to supervising librarian Carrie S. Banks, attendance has more than doubled during the pandemic.

WHAT TO READ THIS WEEKEND

Westinghouse Campus Library
Brooklyn, New York

What to Read This Weekend was a web series recorded live on Friday afternoons by two New York City school librarians: Rachel Chapman (a.k.a. her Instagram moniker, "STEAMLibrarian") of the Westinghouse Educational Campus in Brooklyn and Marie Southwell (a.k.a. "A Salty Librarian") of the Graphic Arts Campus in Manhattan. In each of the 19 episodes recorded from April through August, the pair shared four favorite books on a theme and explained how their students could access them for free. As campus librarians, both Chapman and Southwell were responsible for several schools each and wanted a way to connect with their students during virtual learning. "We really missed doing librarian things in the world of social distancing," Chapman said, "and we found that our students weren't reading because they didn't know how to get access to books. We thought a web series would help show them how to do that." The show was recorded live; the first half was pre-planned and covered themes like poetry, mystery, and LGBTQ+ fiction, sometimes with the help of guest librarians; in the second half, the duo went off air to take students' questions. The show was aired live on Google Hangouts, and the recordings were posted to Instagram TV, YouTube, and their website, which can be found at http://bit.ly/w2rtw2020.

YOUR VIRTUAL FIELD TRIP

Mercer County District Library
Celina, Ohio

With actual school field trips all but canceled, library assistant Remington Hill gave kids the next best thing: a PBS-style documentary series in which Hill traveled with a two-person film crew to places of local interest and recorded the tour that children would be taken on if they were there. The 5- to 15-minute videos—featuring outings to a castle, dairy farm, and exotic reptile expo, just to name a few—correlated to the reading and crafts offered that week in the library's summer reading program. "From comments on the videos, to positive word of mouth, to a few letters I received from the people I met with, I found this was a really great way to keep the community engaged with education even while summer camps and other services weren't being offered in person," Hill said. A few standout memories for Hill: learning to chisel limestone, holding a python, and learning how cows are milked. The videos aired on Friday mornings and are still available on the library's Facebook page.

Online Storytime and Coronavirus: It's Fair Use, Folks

It's been one of the most-asked questions in ALA's Public Programs Office throughout the pandemic. Is it legal to post a recorded storytime on a Facebook or YouTube page? The answer lies in *fair use*, an exception to U.S. copyright law that allows for the use of a protected work without permission.

The 10-second answer is: during a health crisis like COVID-19, online storytimes benefit society more than ever, so your online storytime likely falls within fair use.

Of course, when it comes to legal matters, the devil is in the details. Carrie Russell, copyright specialist in ALA's Public Policy and Advocacy Office, explains the finer points in the interview below.

How does copyright apply to storytime in non-pandemic times?

Storytime is a quintessential service of public and school libraries. Its social benefits are unquestioned as it advances literacy and learning, key by-products of copyright law. When we think of storytime that takes place in the library (a public place) before a group of people, we are exercising the right of *public performance*, an exclusive right of an author, publisher, or other rights holder.

Fair use tells us whether we can exercise that exclusive right without prior permission and still not be infringing the law. It's hard to imagine that a storybook author would say "no, you cannot read the book aloud" or "it'll cost you a royalty fee," especially when the library has purchased the book. It is accepted across the board that reading aloud to children is a fair use. A rights holder could deny you to permission to read a book aloud to children, but to do so would work against the objective of the copyright law. We use fair use to assess whether the socially beneficial use outweighs the economic interest of the rights holder. One could also imagine that fundamental rights that librarians value, such as intellectual freedom, equity of access, and free speech, would be diminished if rights holders had that much control over the use of a work.

Storytime is a quintessential fair use, and there is no need for permission or a licensing fee. The basis of this finding is the consideration of the fair use factors: (1) the purpose of the use, (2) the nature of the publication, (3) the amount of the work used, and (4) the effect on the market for the work. For a full explanation of these factors, visit programminglibrarian.org/fairuse.

What if that storytime is livestreamed or recorded and posted online?

This question is essentially asking if the social benefits of storytime are lost if the storytime is delivered digitally. The social benefits remain the same regardless of the means of delivery, so it makes sense that digital storytime is also fair.

Unfortunately, we do not have the same extent of user rights in the digital environment as in the analog environment. Going digital with a use is always trickier, which is unfortunate and often not good public policy.

There are a few spots where copyright can get dicey with digital storytime. One is that more people will have access to the storytime. Some argue that a larger audience is a problem, and if the storytime is recorded or downloaded, more people can see and hear the storytime repeatedly.

Embellishments like the addition of music may implicate the rights of other rights holders. It's safer to use public domain music or music covered by loose creative commons-type licensing or to skip the music altogether. An exception would be if the music adds significantly to the educational experience of the storytime, which would qualify as fair use.

Another concern is that some publishers now sell storytime videos, so one might argue that one should buy storytime in hopes that the revenue would go to the author and illustrator of the work. A fair use reading might still apply to a digital storytime especially when limited to the library's patrons and not available to everyone all of the time.

Does fair use change in a crisis like the one we face now?

A critical thing to know about fair use is that it is, by design, flexible, so it can accommodate a wide variety of circumstances. The courts have not taken up cases that address the use of copyrighted works to minimize a public health crisis. But we can answer that question by again looking at the four factors of fair use—in particular, the first factor of purpose.

At the worst of the pandemic, the public couldn't access library materials because of widespread library closures. In some places, social distancing is still keeping students out of classrooms, so learning is taking place online. Parents and care-givers are doing more educating in the home.

More than ever, sharing storytimes digitally benefits society, so it falls squarely within fair use.

Recently, we've seen children's book authors come forward on social media to give permission for libraries and teachers to share their books digitally. Is their permission needed?

While it's a nice gesture, authors' permission is not required given the exigent circumstances.

Will the legality of these recordings change after the pandemic ends?

Yes, the fair use argument will not be as strong, but in my opinion, it could still be made depending on other circumstances. For example, in some storytimes, the children engage in part of the public performance by providing aspects or embellishments to the story. For children with disabilities, storytime may have to be modified to meet their needs, which would add to a strong fair use argument.

So, to recap—and with the understanding that you can't give legal advice—how safe is it for libraries to post online storytimes to their webpages or social media channels at the present time?

There is a growing consensus among copyright experts that posting online storytimes to continue mission-driven library and educational services during the coronavirus emergency is a fair use. As always, when using protected resources, I recommend that efforts be taken whenever possible to restrict access and further distribution of the storytime to the public.

NOTES

1. Mary Davis Fournier and Sarah Ostman, eds., *Ask, Listen, Empower: Grounding Your Library Work in Community Engagement* (Chicago: American Library Association, 2020), https://www.alastore.ala.org/content/ask-listen-empower-grounding-your-library -work-community-engagement.

2. Rachael Levy, "Who Are the Proud Boys? The Group Trump Told to 'Stand Back and Stand By,'" *Wall Street Journal*, November 6, 2020, https://www.wsj.com/articles/ who-are-proud-boys-11601485755.

3. John Sides, "The Political Scientist Ray Wolfinger Has Died," *Washington Post*, February 8, 2015, www.washingtonpost.com/news/monkey-cage/wp/2015/02/08/the-political -scientist-ray-wolfinger-has-died/.

CHAPTER TWO

CONVERSATION

Talking was challenging in 2020 given the need for masks and social distancing, but videoconferencing and social media made many, if not all, things possible. In this chapter, we look at community conversations, panel discussions, mental health check-ins, and other methods that libraries used to have the conversations their communities so needed.

CIVILITY IN AMERICA

The Ferguson Library
Stamford, Connecticut

Since 2012, the Ferguson Library's Civility in America series has featured some of the nation's leading thinkers offering their perspectives on what must be done to restore civility in our country. The programs, sponsored by the library, the Dilenschneider Group, and Hearst Media Services, are usually held in person. During the pandemic the library took the program online, using Zoom and streaming live to YouTube. In one program, they spoke with former New York Governor George Pataki to discuss his book *Beyond the Great Divide: How a Nation Became a Neighborhood*, and in another program, they spoke with pharmaceutical and biotech executive Dr. Clive Meanwell on coronavirus and other pandemics and their impact on civility. "While the talks in both cases were very interesting, it was the interactive Q&A section that was fantastic," said library president Alice Knapp. "Since people had to type in the questions, the monologues were eliminated and the questions were direct." While the chat was a perk, it was also a drawback: the anonymity of the chat function meant that people were less civil with their questions, especially in Governor Pataki's talk. "Luckily, he wasn't tech savvy and never saw those comments," Knapp said.

COLD SPRING CHATS

Julia L. Butterfield Memorial Library
Cold Spring, New York

Overlooking the Hudson River, Cold Spring, New York, is a scenic village of 2,000 located an hour northwest of Manhattan. The community has retained its quaint character despite the changing times; "this is largely due to the steadfast loyalty of the Cold Spring residents," the village website states, "and their ingenuity in adapting to the needs of the present while carefully preserving their heritage and way of life."[1] Library director Gillian Murphy saw an opportunity to build on that heritage during the pandemic. In a five-part Zoom series, she interviewed longtime residents of Cold Spring. "I love old history. I grew up here," Murphy said. "I have some of my own stories, but they're of a different generation. I'm trying to get anybody from the '40s, '50s, '60s, '70s, '80s, so we can get a look at what the community was like at all those different times." Interviewees were regular folks—the high school Spanish teacher, a postal worker, and longtime community volunteers—who discussed how their families came to Cold Spring and what the village was like in years past. The interviews were shared on Facebook and received hundreds of views.

COMMUNITY CONVERSATIONS:
HOW HAVE YOU EXPERIENCED COVID-19?

Garfield County Public Library District
Rifle, Colorado

When they set out to host a community conversation about how residents were experiencing the pandemic, Garfield County Public Library District staff knew it was vital that they make the event bilingual. They hired local professional interpreters (a $360 cost for two interpreters for two hours) and used Zoom's language interpretation features. The conversation was facilitated by trained volunteer community leader/facilitators from local grassroots organization Mountain Voices Project. Several participants were part of local grassroots organization Madres en Acción (Mothers in Action). After an introduction, the conversation began with each of the 12 community members in attendance sharing their story in two minutes or less. After everyone shared, facilitators summarized the commonalities they had heard and asked each person to share a word or phrase about how they felt after hearing one another's stories. "Most people said they were grateful to be included and heard, grateful to feel not so alone, grateful that people were honest about the difficulties," said Lisa Detweiler, the library's interim events coordinator. "The purpose of the conversation was to listen to each other, not to name or solve problems."

New to Facilitating Virtual Conversations? Get to Know the Technology[2]

As you prepare for your videoconference, you should familiarize yourself with the following technical features:

Recording: Most platforms allow for recording (sometimes with a fee). If you are recording a session, you should say so at the beginning of the meeting in case anyone would like to opt out of participating. In addition to informing participants, share how the recording will be used and if it will be shared with participants or anywhere else. Noting this ahead of time, in the invitation, is ideal.

Muting: All platforms include muting capabilities, which can be managed by the host, participants, or both. Read up on the options and how to change the settings. In small conversations, it may work to have everyone unmuted, but as the conversation gets larger, you may wish to set a "question-and-answer" mode that mutes all participants but gives them the ability to unmute when they wish to speak. This avoids background noises while others are speaking. Make sure to go over the process of muting and unmuting at the start of your meeting.

Chat: The chat function allows for another communication method. This tool is helpful for sharing information or instructions with participants, including ground rules, questions, or links. It can be distracting if used for side conversations. As the facilitator, make it clear at the start of the conversation if you would like participants to use the chat box freely or only for specific needs.

Breakouts: If you expect a large turnout for your conversation, you may wish to use breakout rooms to allow participants to meet in smaller groups. Generally, virtual conversations seem to work best with groups of six to twelve; when you find yourself with larger groups, breaking them into smaller groups can help create more connection and deepen the conversation. You may wish to recruit additional facilitators to join each breakout group. If the breakout groups won't each have a facilitator, provide instructions so people know what to discuss in the breakouts and what they will be asked to share upon returning to the larger group.

Screen sharing: When conversations involve presenting facts or figures, or if a guest speaker is joining you, you may wish to use screen sharing to present slides, documents, or video. If this is not available, you could send participants links to the documents in advance and ask that they have them available for the event, or review them prior to the conversation start.

Identification: Whenever possible, ask participants to join the event using their first name so they are easy to identify. You can also ask people to share their location or preferred pronouns. If you have different topics for breakout rooms, you can use this feature to sort people into groups by requesting participants add a number or the name of the topic into their name field. That way you can easily sort groups by their topic of interest.

DOWN TIME WITH CRANSTON PUBLIC LIBRARY

Oak Lawn Branch Library, Cranston Public Library
Cranston, Rhode Island

Down Time with Cranston Public Library is a podcast where library staff, and sometimes special guests, talk about what they're reading, watching, and doing during these times. Branch librarian Tayla Cardillo started the podcast in April 2020 as a way to help patrons feel connected to the library when they couldn't physically come to the library during a state stay-at-home order; once she released the first episode with two colleagues, staff from across the system were eager to participate. Each episode runs about 45 minutes, and topics have ranged from positive apocalyptic stories to favorite queer books and movies to flea markets. "When I started the show, I thought of it as a way to take some of the interactions that we frequently have with patrons in the library and bring them into their homes," Cardillo says. "But it has grown to be so much more than that. It's been a vehicle for us to raise up the voices of under-represented groups in our community and to raise awareness about timely issues." Episodes are available on most podcast apps and at anchor. fm/down-time-cpl.

FINDING HOPE: INTERFAITH GROUP DISCUSSION

Gail Borden Public Library
Elgin, Illinois

Gail Borden Public Library serves nearly 150,000 residents in the northwest suburbs of Chicago. In the midst of the COVID-19 health crisis and the social unrest in response to racial inequities, the library hosted a panel discussion to help residents find hope. The June 2020 virtual event included five speakers from different faith traditions—an atheist, a Buddhist, a Christian, a Jew, and a Muslim—discussing ways to cope in these difficult times and finding common ground. "It was such a good feeling to be able to provide a meaningful and pertinent program for our patrons," said public programs coordinator Sadia Ahmed. "The response was all positive, and the results of a poll show they wanted more programs like this." Forty-five people attended the Sunday afternoon Zoom program.

GREAT DECISIONS DISCUSSION GROUP

Attleboro Public Library
Attleboro, Massachusetts

Created by the Foreign Policy Association, Great Decisions is a discussion program about world affairs in which participants read a briefing book, watch videos, and meet in a group to discuss some of the most critical global issues facing the United States today. Attleboro Public Library hosted a series of eight group meetings via Zoom starting in early April. "We had planned to start in-person sessions at the end of March when our library suddenly closed, so we took the group online with our current registrants and added a few more," said library director Christine M. Johnson, who facilitated the discussions. "Our participants were very excited to be able to interact socially during this stressful time, and our discussions were vibrant." The Great Decisions for 2020 included climate change and the global order, India and Pakistan, and artificial intelligence and data. Meetings lasted around 75 minutes each, and an average of eight participants attended each session. Participants paid for their own $32 briefing books from the Foreign Policy Association; because they had already been ordered for registered participants when the library closed, the library's assistant director delivered them to homes.

THE PAGES OF MADISON COUNTY

Jackson-Madison County Library
Jackson, Tennessee

After a summer of reduced hours and social distancing, librarians at Jackson-Madison County Library were looking to connect their patrons in a new way. They were also looking to get rid of a large stack of empty journals that had gone unused from a summer program. A collaborative journaling program, The Pages of Madison County, accomplished both. Forty journals are available for check-out at the library, with themes including Netflix recommendations, be the change, and stories my grandparents told me. Each journal comes with a theme and a page of instructions. Some are ongoing stories that each person can add to; others are spaces for sharing funny stories or bragging about grandkids. "We're not looking for great literature and art here," says librarian Jennifer Brewer. "This is just for fun. We just want you to write whatever comes to your mind, sketch whatever comes to your mind, have fun sharing with other people in our community." The library plans to shelve the journals when they are completed; for now, they are in a special display.

QUARANTINE BRUNCH

Queens Public Library
Queens, New York

In the '80s and '90s, DJ Ralph McDaniels introduced hip-hop fans to emerging artists as co-host of *Video Music Box* on New York's public television station, WNYC-TV. Today, McDaniels spreads that love as hip-hop coordinator at Queens Public Library, where he builds relationships within the hip-hop community and organizes programming ranging from celebrity talks to graffiti workshops. He also leads an Instagram Live chat, where he spins vinyl, interviews guests, and invites comments from listeners. On Saturday afternoons during lockdown, McDaniels's program took on the name of Quarantine Brunch. Starting on March 31, he broadcast a curated DJ set and interviewed local leaders and speakers. On June 2, following the police killing of George Floyd in Minneapolis, McDaniels turned off the music and chatted about fears, challenges, and hope in the community. More than 10,000 viewers from all over the world—most of whom are new to Queens Public Library programs—have tuned in to dozens of livestreams.. "What's awesome about our live programs at Queens Public Library is we now have folks from all over the world streaming, watching, and chatting in real time," says the library's data and project coordinator Jill Anderson.

SOCRATES CAFÉ

Allentown Public Library
Allentown, Pennsylvania

Based on the book and method developed by Christopher Phillips, Socrates Café uses the Socratic Method to discuss an agreed-upon topic. From April to June 2020, Allentown Public Library hosted two virtual cafés each month. At each meet-up, participants discussed a question of the day. Attendees could submit an anonymous question to the discussion leader in the chat box upon arrival, and everyone voted to determine which question to discuss. Doing the discussions via Zoom required some technical finessing; participants were asked to either click "raise hand" or to chat the librarian to be called on to speak. Like the in-person cafés, participants are encouraged to listen to each other's ideas and respond with their own thoughts on the topic when called upon. "You'll quickly learn that one question often leads to many others, so you never know where it might lead," the event description reads. "Don't worry, if you get too far off topic, we'll eventually reel it back in." Between five and fourteen people attended each café, which was a pleasant surprise for librarians who didn't know what to expect. "This was our first real go at a virtual program," said library director Renee Haines. "Just the fact that we had consistent interest and participation was surprise enough."

TAKE A DEEP BREATH

El Dorado County Library
Placerville, California

The big world events happening around us can have an outsized impact on young people. Once a week on Monday afternoons, El Dorado County Library hosts a teen mental health club by videoconference to give teens a chance to chat, unwind, and learn about mental health. Club members are joined by a community health advocate who bonds with the teens and helps guide them toward any local resources they may need. While it's a small group—usually five or so teens attend—the relationships are meaningful, and the teens have started to take leadership roles within the club and sharing their own ideas for self-care and stress management. "What stands out to me most are the times that teens find someone else in their community that is experiencing the same feelings that they are," says youth services librarian Ashleigh Torres.

Facilitating a Group Conversation

Leading discussion-based programs can be stressful. Whether your book club is marred by lengthy silences or your teen advisory board meetings are out of control, check out the following tips for leading your best online discussions, developed in consultation with the National Coalition for Dialogue and Deliberation.

Open the room early for people who don't know the platform. We recommend that the host arrive at least 15 minutes before start time—especially if some participants are new to the technology. Invite folks to join early if they need any help.

Set ground rules. Ground rules are a list of terms that participants agree to follow—and the facilitator agrees to uphold—during a conversation. They help establish expectations for how people will talk with one another and offer a tool for helping to maintain open communication. There is no one set list of ground rules that facilitators should follow; rules can be adapted to the situation, and participants can help create or modify them. Get agreement from participants though a verbal "yes," a thumbs up, or another way.

Call on participants or set up a routine for who speaks when. Awkward silences happen in person, but they can feel especially pronounced when everyone is staring at their screens. In virtual settings, you may need to be more involved in calling on participants or setting up a routine for who speaks when. One option is to start with a round where everyone has the chance to speak in order. This order can be used consistently through the program or just when it seems helpful to manage talking over one another.

Give people the option to pass. If you're calling on people to speak, some attendees may feel like they're being put on the spot. Make sure participants know that they can always "pass."

Limit your screen sharing. In some platforms, screen sharing makes it difficult to see people's faces; participants' faces get pushed to the side to make room for the shared document. Try not to leave a document shared for longer than is necessary because the static image may cause people to disengage.

TALK IT OUT

Piscataway Public Library
Piscataway, New Jersey

The multiple crises of 2020 challenged the mental health of countless Americans, and teens were no exception. "It's more important than ever to check in with our teens and give them a confidential space to talk about these issues," says teen services librarian Kate-Lynn Brown. Brown runs Piscataway Public Library's Talk It Out program, an award-winning program that has been a staple in her community since 2017. By connecting teens with community partners like the Piscataway Township Violence Crisis Intervention Team or the Middlesex County Center for Empowerment, Talk It Out fills a service gap for teens while helping them learn to self-regulate, be more independent, think critically, communicate, and problem solve. Before the pandemic, the program met in person in the library's teen space, which serves as a hangout for two nearby middle schools. The club has kept going strong after it moved online, discussing gender norms in teen dating, anxiety and depression, and how to cope with stress in difficult times. "We've also been focusing on activities teens do for mental health breaks, and in that vein, have given them some breaks by playing Kahoot or other online games during some session," Brown said. On June 1, 2020, after the killing of George Floyd, a social worker from the Center for Empowerment led the teens in a discussion. "They shared their thoughts and frustrations, asked questions, and left with resources detailing how they could help," Brown said. The program is held each Monday at 3 p.m.

TEEN VIRTUAL HANGOUT

Half Hollow Hills Community Library
Dix Hills, New York

When families in the Long Island hamlet of Dix Hills were socially distancing, teen librarians offered a series of teen virtual hangouts on Zoom to give them a social outlet. "The idea was to give them a chance to see their friends, see us, and blow off some steam," said children's librarian Liz Hughes. Also in attendance was a social worker to answer any questions the teens had about mental health. Hughes was surprised to see how popular it was; nearly 20 teens attended. "The teens loved it," she said. "We were amazed at how into the idea they were and how much they participated."

NOTES

1. "About the Village," Village of Cold Spring, New York, https://www.coldspringny.gov/home/pages/about-village.

2. This resource has been adapted from "Libraries Transforming Communities: Leading Conversations in Small and Rural Libraries Facilitation Guide," ALA Public Programs Office, September 2020, http://www.ala.org/tools/sites/ala.org.tools/files/content/PPO_LTC_Fac_Guide%20-%20revised%20v3.pdf, 31–32.

CHAPTER THREE

CONNECTION

For many Americans, particularly the most vulnerable, COVID-19 meant crushing isolation. Libraries served as a connecting force during these times, hosting get-togethers big and small, serious and trivial, to remind people that they weren't alone. Others delivered books, organized letters for the elderly, or helped people take a breath.

AUTISM-FRIENDLY CONCERTS

Brooklyn Public Library
Brooklyn, New York

The nonprofit Music for Autism seeks to expose people with autism and their families to high-quality music performed in an environment where individual differences are celebrated and where no one will be embarrassed. Their concerts feature professional musicians, including Tony Award winners, Grammy-nominated classical artists, and Pulitzer Prize winners. Brooklyn Public Library has partnered with Music for Autism to host quarterly concerts in-person for the past eight years; during the pandemic, the library began promoting Music for Autism's biweekly virtual concerts through their events calendar. Registration was required, and participants received a link to a YouTube livestream one hour before the event.

BENSON ONLINE BOOK CLUB

Benson Memorial Library
Titusville, Pennsylvania

Benson Memorial Library's answer to a pandemic book club was a Facebook event page. Participants were invited to drop by the page at any time on Fridays, when executive director Jessica Hilburn would post between five and nine general book questions to spark conversation. There was no communal read; posters chatted about what they were currently reading and general likes and dislikes. "People have been able to network and socialize with others they've never met before over their shared love of books," Hilburn said. During the second week of the online club, Hilburn received a Facebook message from an essential worker who thanked her for offering the program and giving them a chance to relax. A challenge was keeping the questions fresh. "After weeks or months of doing an online book club with no specific book, it was tough to come up with new questions, but participants loved the event so much they send me their ideas for questions, which keeps it fresh!" From the online club's start in March until its last e-gathering in August, they discussed 108 questions. A few favorites: What was your favorite book when you were a child? Has a book ever made you cry or laugh out loud? If so, which book? How do you treat your books? Dog ear the pages? Bend the spine? Use bookmarks?

BOOKFIX

St. Ignatius College Prep
San Francisco, California

With campus closed and their 1,500 middle and high school students learning remotely, librarians Cara Brancoli and Christina Wenger set out to find a fun way to lift spirits, promote reading, and get to know their patrons' reading interests better. They did all three things in one fell swoop with BookFix, a book subscription service she created inspired by the clothing subscription box company Stitch Fix. To participate in BookFix, a patron—be it a student, teacher, administrator, or staff—takes a personal style quiz on the BookFix website. The librarians then handpick three books and send them directly to the patron's home mailbox. When they're done—whether they read the books or not—the patron simply returns the book to the library by mail using a prepaid included return label. When they're ready for more books, they submit a feedback form online and get a new batch. No commitment is necessary; participants can start and stop as they like.

BOOK JAM

Princeton Public Library
Princeton, New Jersey

Since 2006, the Princeton Children's Book Festival attracted hordes of book lovers to the plaza outside Princeton Public Library on an autumn Saturday each year. For obvious reasons, the library decided to cancel the in-person book festival in 2020, instead offering a virtual book jam. The library's youth services department, other staff, and the festival sponsor, jaZam's, began brainstorming in May for the September event. "We realized that we didn't want the event to just be people talking," said manager of adult programming Janie Hermann. "We wanted it to be interactive, creative, and outside of the box. Susan Conlon and the rest of the planning team worked really hard on that." The event plans went through several iterations before the team landed on a final vision: a one-day Crowdcast event with children's authors and illustrators talking and engaging with the audience throughout the day. There was an Illustrator Sketch-Off, where audience members submitted prompts for a panel of illustrators to draw on the spot; Reading with Pride, a panel featuring authors who have written about the LGBTQ+ experience; Animal Antics, with picture-book authors that included a wacky animal-themed game of "Would You Rather?"; and A Funny Thing Happened on the Way to the Book Jam, in which three middle-grade authors joined forces to write an interactive story with help from the audience. Twelve library staff members were involved in the live presentations, including an on-camera host and a tech person for each of the six sessions. "It was fabulous. Even more successful than we thought it would be," Hermann said.

Moderating Virtual Author Talks: Seven Tips

If you've hosted an author talk or moderated a panel discussion in person, rest assured: online, the drill is pretty similar.

"Nothing is more important than preparation," says Donna Seaman, Booklist's adult books editor and an award-winning literary critic who has interviewed hundreds of authors throughout her career. "The more fluent you are in the writer's work, the better the conversation."

Still, Seaman cautions, you may need to make a few adjustments in a virtual setting. Here are her top seven suggestions:

1. **Plan for Q&A.** The question-and-answer section can have a lot of moving pieces, so you'll want a plan. Some platforms, like Zoom, have separate features for chat and Q&A. Seaman asks attendees to type informal messages and greetings into the chat box, reserving the Q&A feature for questions that people would like her to ask publicly. Recruit helpers to monitor those features, if possible, so you can focus on the conversation. "It makes me nervous to switch my screen back and forth, so I ask someone to text me the questions on my phone or a tablet. It can be comforting to have a second device," Seaman says.

2. **Meet early to check tech.** When you invite an author, explain the technical requirements for your event (e.g., a laptop/desktop with a camera, a good internet connection) and ask if they know how to use the platform. On the day of, Seaman suggests meeting the author in your virtual space at least 20 minutes before start time to check audio and video, "just as you would do a sound-check in an auditorium." This is also a good time to practice muting and unmuting and turning video on and off.

3. **Be a set designer.** Before you begin, take a few minutes to (gently) tweak the author's surroundings so they are well lit and have a flattering background. "You want it to look professional," Seaman says. "On the other hand, the audience likes to see the speaker's home. You want a mix of intimate and polished." The same goes for your space.

4. **Know that you're being watched.** (No pressure, right?) "When you're on stage moderating a live event you can safely assume most people are looking at the author," Seaman says, "and you're at a distance. But when you're on screen in close-up, you have to be very aware of what you're doing." That means doing your best to curb nervous tics like fidgeting or licking your lips and avoiding

the temptation to frequently fix your hair or adjust your clothing.

5. **Be succinct.** "Online, time is really precious," Seaman says. Without the energy of a room full of people, your audience is likely to get distracted if your conversation meanders. Make good use of your screen time by keeping introductions crisp and moving the conversation along. At the same time, it's also important to . . .

6. **Pause before responding.** In a virtual setting, answers to your questions may be a bit delayed due to the internet connection. Make sure the author has finished talking before you jump in. "You have to learn to give it a beat to let the author respond. If you notice you're talking over them, give it two beats," Seaman says.

7. **Create clear segues between speakers.** If you're moderating a panel, encourage speakers to mute themselves when they aren't talking, but be aware that they may need a few seconds to unmute when it's their turn to speak. You can lessen the awkwardness by giving a casual heads-up, such as "I have a question for you now, Natalie, if you could please unmute yourself."

DEAR FRIEND: QUARANTINE PEN PAL CAMPAIGN

Germantown Community Library
Germantown, Tennessee

Like cities and towns all over the world, city leaders in Germantown, Tennessee, put their heads together early in the pandemic to try to plan an effective response to the virus, both in terms of health and the isolation it caused. As a result, they reached out to staff at the Germantown Community Library, and together they created a traditional pen pal letter–writing program to help quarantined young people connect with homebound senior citizens. Patrons could sign up online, and staff also conducted outreach through phone calls, letters, printed fliers, and connections with local senior living facilities. "The program has been tremendously helpful to provide youth and senior citizens a way to stay active and connected during a tumultuous time for the whole world," says library director Daniel Page. More than 100 participants signed up in the first month.

DRIVING WHILE BLACK WITH DR. GRETCHEN SORIN

Piscataway Public Library
Piscataway, New Jersey

Piscataway Public Library's Juneteenth 2020 program came about seren-dipitously when a book chat participant recommended *Driving While Black: African American Travel and the Road to Civil Rights* and offered to connect the library to its author, Dr. Gretchen Sorin. The book and a corresponding PBS documentary explore how automobiles fundamentally changed African American life. "At first, we hesitated to do the program virtually, thinking we could attract a larger audience in person," recalls adult services librarian Joy Robinson, "but as the pandemic continued and then Ahmaud Arbery was killed, we decided to seize the moment and the opportunity to call attention to the other epidemic everyone seemed to be ignoring: Black people were still being killed with impunity in America. Tying the discussion to a commem-oration of Juneteenth seemed most appropriate." No one could foresee that between scheduling the event and its June 17 program date, the topic would sadly become even more relevant with the police killing of George Floyd that sparked national protests. In a Zoom conversation, Sorin and filmmakers Ric Burns and Emir Lewis discussed the history of the automobile and the transgressive power it afforded Blacks to travel into formerly whites-only spaces. The discussion also delved into how the phrase "driving while Black" relates to incidents of Black motorists being stopped and killed by police. The library partnered with the Piscataway African American Seniors Club to promote the program and 130 people logged in to the event, the library's largest virtual program to date. "I learned not to hesitate when something wonderful drops into your lap just because it doesn't feel 'earned,'" Robinson says, "and that taking risks can bring immeasurable rewards that benefit my entire community." The speakers later returned for another virtual program after the film premiered in October 2020.

FIFTH ANNUAL ASIAN-PACIFIC AMERICAN HERITAGE CELEBRATION AT HOME

Gail Borden Public Library District
Elgin, Illinois

For the past four years, Gail Borden Public Library District has celebrated Asian Pacific American Heritage Month with an in-person festival at the library with speakers, performers, authors, and crafts. Instead of canceling altogether when COVID-19 struck, the library reached out to its event committee, which was "delighted" to bring the event online. "We can build resilience through joy and celebration with community," community collaboration coordinator Danielle Henson says. "If you find yourself in a pandemic and working from home and you might have to cancel an important festival or large event that is important to you and your community, gather your partners and coworkers and think again." Partner organizations, presenters, and staff filmed video clips with cooking demos, bilingual storytelling, dance lessons, origami instructions, history lessons, and more, and they submitted them to the library to edit and curate into an online festival. The videos streamed back-to-back for three hours on the library's Facebook page on May 16, and they remain curated online. "We connected and celebrated community at a time when we needed joy and wonder the most," Henson says.

FUN WITH RAINBOW THERAPY DOGS

Skokie Public Library
Skokie, Illinois

Before COVID-19, Skokie Public Library conducted a monthly program for kids with disabilities called Rainbow Therapy Time. Working with therapy dogs from a Chicago-area nonprofit, kids interacted with trained therapy dogs with the help of dog handlers and library volunteers. In the process, the children strengthened verbal, motor, cognitive, and social skills, including confidence and independence. When the pandemic shuttered the library in March 2020, community engagement supervisor Holly Jin became concerned about the lack of opportunities for children with special needs, so she created a remote version of the program. Families log on to Zoom from home and spend 30 minutes online with the dogs and their owners, using breakout rooms to separately interact with the dogs simultaneously. Visual materials, such as choice boards and common dog commands, are e-mailed to participants ahead of time. "Activities have obviously been modified, but each child has the opportunity to interact with the dogs, doing so in ways they had not done in person," Jin says. For example, one child used her augmentative communication device—which she doesn't bring in person to the library—to speak to the dogs and their handlers. The therapy dog organization, Rainbow Animal Assisted Therapy, said that doing the therapy via videoconference had opened opportunities for them: "Our hospital partners, especially pediatric child life specialists, are intrigued by the idea and moving ahead with presenting the concept to administration. . . .This concept may also work in some school settings. All these opportunities are an outgrowth of [Skokie Public Library's] program." After the first session, a child's mother e-mailed the library: "In all this uncertainty it was just so good to see the cute puppies and friends. It made us all feel 'normal' for the moment. It was huge!"

GROWN-UP STORY TIME

Tyler Public Library
Tyler, Texas

Grown-Up Story Time is a series of videos—usually less than ten minutes each—of a public domain story, poem, or book selection read by a Tyler Public Library employee that is posted to the library's Facebook page. The library has found that it's a fun way to connect with patrons, and by inviting guest readers from across City Hall, it also helps forge connections to other city departments. "We had our city manager read the Gettysburg Address and a history for Memorial Day," said reference associate T. J. Rankin. "It's also a great way to highlight the talents of your staff; for example, we put up a storytime of the windmill scene from Don Quixote, read in its original language by one of our Latinx staff members." The video generally displays a still image while an employee reads their selection; staff creates the videos using Headliner, a browser-based video platform.

GUIDED MEDITATION

Prince George's County Memorial Library System
Prince George's County, Maryland

During a phenomenally stressful time, Prince George's County Memorial Library System reminded their Facebook followers to slow down and connect with their breath. On some Friday afternoons, Will Froliklong, a staff member with guided meditation experience, leads an easy guided meditation designed to be calming and stress reducing. It also helps promote personal connection. "Before we begin, I want to acknowledge that these are hard times," he says in the October 16 meditation, filming from his home. "Globally we are experiencing a pandemic. Nationally our country is having a long overdue conversation about racial justice. Meditation can be a tool to relieve tension and stress but also a tool for resilience, fortifying our bodies and our minds for our collective work toward change." Over the following ten minutes or so, he speaks in a soothing voice, encouraging viewers to close their eyes, release tension, and simply be still. "It has been a great addition to our program line-up [since] dealing with the stress of a public health emergency," says public services manager Rachel Zukowski.

JUNIOR VIRTUAL ART SHOW

Woodstock Public Library, Sequoyah Regional Library System
Woodstock, Georgia

Woodstock Public Library had wanted to create an in-person junior art show in the library's community room, but when the library closed for safety reasons that plan went out the window. So youth services associate Jennifer Brooks pivoted and decided to display the talents of young artists in Woodstock in a virtual art show. Patrons under 18 were invited to create a piece of art and share photos of it with staff via e-mail. They asked for one close-up photo of their art and one of them holding their art, and had the youth submit the photos along with a Google Form explaining their masterpieces. Brooks created the show in a Google Slide presentation and posted a link to it on the library's social media accounts. When a viewer "enters" the art show, they see a stark white gallery-like display with the framed artwork hung on the virtual walls with the artist's first name and age listed below it. "I wanted to make it as realistic and participatory as possible," Brooks said. Eight kids participated (with some kids submitting multiple pieces), ranging in age from three to twelve, and each received a certificate naming them an "Artist Extraordinaire."

KK'S VIRTUAL STORYTIME

Marshes of Glynn Libraries
Brunswick, Georgia

A familiar face goes a long way when times are tough. During the pandemic, libraries across the country found a silver lining by using technology to reconnect with old favorites. Kelly Greene, a.k.a. Ms. K.K., was a beloved storytime reader at Georgia's Marshes of Glynn Libraries before she and her family moved eight hours away in late 2019. With COVID, the library invited Ms. K.K. back to do a weekly storytime on Facebook Live. "Our community has been thrilled to be able to connect with K.K. again," said programming coordinator Diana Graham. "Not only does this provide a wonderful service for families who are still hesitant to attend in-person storytimes, but it also makes storytime accessible to children with disabilities or autoimmune diseases." The partnership did require some pre-planning. K.K.'s local library was also closed during the shutdown, so Marshes of Glynn library staff shipped her packages of books in advance. Over Thanksgiving break, Ms. K.K. planned to visit in person and lead an outdoor, socially distanced storytime.

KNITTING GROUP

McArthur Public Library
Biddeford, Maine

Longtime library interest groups became a virtual solace for many during periods of isolation. One in-person knitting group at McArthur Public Library, located just south of Portland on the coast of Maine, had been meeting since 2015 under the leadership of adult services supervisor and librarian Melanie

Taylor Coombs. In mid-March 2020, the library was forced to close, and the group moved online. Regular knitters plus participants from around the country started to join their gathering on the Jitsi platform each Friday at 10 a.m. The group was even contacted by someone in Japan wishing to create a similar program. "Knitting is universal and welcoming. The Friday morning meetings have always been about people getting together and socializing," Coombs says. "It was needed during the pandemic more than ever."

QUARANZINE (A QUARANTINE ZINE)

Arlington Public Library
Arlington, Virginia

Quaranzine was a small online publication of local art and writing by the Arlington community, distributed through the library website. Launched in the early days of the pandemic in April 2020, Quaranzine was based on the DIY (do-it-yourself) aesthetic of zines and shares creative works that document how residents responded to quarantine. "The idea was to offer people a platform to share the projects they've been undertaking while quarantined at home and to document the strange time we found ourselves in," said programming and partnerships librarian Liz Laribee. "It was a way to reimagine the library as a gathering place, virtually." The project began with an edition composed of pieces by Arlington County staff; it was posted on the library website alongside a call for submissions from the larger community so people had an idea of what to submit. Submissions included art, writing (essays, poetry, fiction, top-ten lists, reviews, etc.), visual tutorials, comics, photography, and recipes. Arlington Public Library created ten issues of Quaranzine between April and July 2020, publishing about 20 submissions per issue. You can read more about the project at programminglibrarian .org/quaranzine.

SPRING ART SHOW FOR ALL AGES

Boyertown Community Library
Boyertown, Pennsylvania

Youth services coordinator Lisa Rand was eager to find a way for the library
to lift the spirits of residents in her small Pennsylvania town, so she created
a spring art show. All Boyertown community members, regardless of age or
ability, were invited to share artwork in any medium with the library. Twen-
ty-one artists contributed, representing all age groups (preschool to adult)
and a variety of media (pencil, oil, acrylic, ink, watercolor, mixed media, oil
pastels, and photography). Rand used Canva to present the submissions in a
video that was shared on social media, receiving hundreds of views. "The art
show served as a reminder to the community that, even under challenging
conditions, we are capable of creativity, a hopeful spirit, and uplifting one
another," Rand said.

"SPRING FLOWERS" WATERCOLOR ART QUILT BY THE WATERCOLOR COLLABORATIVE

Montclair Community Library, Prince William Public Library System
Dumfries, Virginia

Montclair Community Library's Watercolor Collaborative is a class of intermediate to advanced artists who are led by a volunteer professional teacher
for weekly in-person classes at the library. When the library suddenly closed,
senior librarian Lena Gonzalez Berrios asked the artists to keep painting from
home and submit a piece under the theme "spring flowers" to assemble a virtual watercolor quilt. The assignment was so successful that it led to a virtual
watercolor class offered throughout the summer. The library is also planning
to do a digital quilt each season going forward. "When I proposed the idea, I
wasn't sure if anyone would submit a watercolor piece so that we could bring
it to fruition or if they would be willing to try a virtual class," Berrios said.
"This has been a beautiful model for how community is created not only at
the library but by the library." Berrios also noticed that the project elicited
goodwill for the library as patrons saw the library was doing everything it
could to keep people connected through a difficult time.

STAY AT HOME BOOK CLUB

Fort Worth Public Library
Fort Worth, Texas

The Stay at Home Book Club is for Fort Worth residents and library patrons who are interested in being part of a virtual book club. "You can stay home, and still find community with fellow book lovers right here!" the Facebook group-based club says. Created by adult services manager Jana Hill, the club was launched the day before the Fort Worth Public Library closed due to county stay-at-home orders in March 2020. Unlike all of the library's other book clubs, Stay at Home is entirely asynchronous; Hill runs a poll every few weeks to let members vote on the next read, which is always available as an e-book with plenty of concurrent checkouts. "It's a little challenging to get a feel for how often we need to move on to a new book," Hill says. "Book clubs with actual meetings go on a firm schedule, whereas this group is a little looser." When she gets the sense that members are ready, Hill sets a date for a "meeting" and posts discussion questions about the book. With more than 450 members as of October 2020, the group has reached a new audience that wasn't attending in-person programs. And it happened at a time when readers needed to feel connected. "I feel like I've made new friends and am a little less lonely as a result of the Stay at Home Book Club and the Fort Worth Public Library as a whole," club member Melyssa Prince told *Fort Worth Magazine* in July 2020.[1]

Seven Platforms for Your Virtual Book Club

For many libraries, virtual book clubs have provided a way for readers to make social connections and try to make sense of the world during a time of crisis. But with so many platforms to choose from, making the transition from in-person to online gatherings can be stressful. Here, Ruth Monnier, learning outreach librarian at the Leonard H. Axe Library at Pittsburg State University in Kansas, outlines the strengths and weaknesses of some of the more popular options:

1. **Zoom** gives you 40 minutes per video call with their free version. Currently, 100 participants are allowed at one time. In addition to voice capability, Zoom offers a chat feature for people who may want to type their contributions. Participants

do not need to have a Zoom account and can join via phone, desktop, or tablet. Zoom meetings can be recorded, which is helpful for sharing sessions with participants later. (Participants can decide to not allow their video or audio to be captured.) The facilitator has the ability to mute participants, which is important for individuals unfamiliar with the software as well as to cut down on any echo effects. Please note that Zoom can share the data that it collects with third parties.

2. **Google Meet**, another video-calling app, is part of the G Suite. Based on recent security changes, both facilitators and participants now need to create or sign into an existing Google account to use the platform. Meetings are limited to 60 minutes and 100 participants with no recording option unless the facilitator is part of G Suite Enterprise (Education, Business, etc.). However, there are no limits to the number of meetings you can have. The facilitator can mute, pin, or remove participants. Google Meet does allow for live captioning in English during meetings. Note that Google Meets are encrypted in transit versus end-to-end encryption, which means the information shared via the app lives on Google's servers.

3. **Facebook Live** is a user-friendly option for participants, and anyone can watch, making it a good choice for libraries with Facebook pages. However, the sole focus is on the presenter; participants are not visible and can only add reactions and comments, which limits interaction. Please note that participants should expect all of the privacy (or lack thereof) that they usually receive from Facebook when using the platform.

4. **Instagram Live** is comparable to Facebook Live in that it is a user-friendly option and requires no additional setup if a library has an account. Again, the focus is on the presenter, and there is limited participant interaction. However, Instagram Live participants do need to have an account to access any content and discussion. Please note that Instagram is owned by Facebook and participants have comparable rights to privacy.

5. **Facebook Groups** are free to create as a part of your (or your library's) Facebook account. If you create a "closed" group, participants must have a Facebook account and request membership in the group to join. My virtual long-term weekly book club, Gorilla Alumni Book Club, is hosted via a closed Facebook group set up as a "social learning group." This setup allows me to have "units," which are great for organizing individual book discussions.

6. **Goodreads Groups** function like basic discussion boards and have very limited features, which can be a good thing; they lessen the intimidation factor for less tech-savvy participants. Participants must have a Goodreads account to engage in discussion, but accounts are free for both facilitators and participants. Moderators can create folders for each book and then post individual questions within the folder. Jenn Wigle, adult services coordinator of the Montgomery County Memorial Library System in Texas, and her colleague, reference librarian Molly Bullard, run a Goodreads book club called Fresh*Reads. One quirk they don't love about Goodreads: the most recent user comment automatically rises to the top of the folder, not the most recently asked moderator question. Please note that the current Goodreads Privacy Policy states that they will not rent or sell personally identifiable information to others.

7. **Your library's webpage**, depending on how dynamic it is, can also be a good place to host your book club. Book club members participate by commenting on your discussion. You have full control over members' privacy and how the data is being used. As an example, check out Greene County Public Library in Ohio. Erin Kloosterman, adult services librarian and moderator of their website-based online book club (https://greenelibrary.info/online-book-club/), recommends adding supplemental videos and links into the discussion to deepen members' understanding. That way, members have the option to go more in-depth on their time.

TEENS AND COVID-19: A TOWN HALL MEETING

Half Hollow Hills Community Library
Dix Hills, New York

Teens experienced a summer unlike any other in 2020. Early that summer, Half Hollow Hills Community Library partnered with other area libraries to give teens and their families a much-needed chance to connect with their elected officials about some of the issues most on their minds. In a virtual town hall meeting with a state legislator and city councilman, teens from Huntington Township learned how to stay safe and act responsibly. The Zoom program included a Q&A where teens and their parents had the opportunity to ask questions and express concerns about COVID-19. Teens could earn one community service hour for attending. "It was a lot of work, but the impact and payoff of the program made it all worth it in the end," said children's librarian Liz Hughes.

A THOUSAND WORDS

New Hanover County Public Library
Wilmington, North Carolina

In May 2020, library assistant Colette Strassburg began posting a call for photo submissions on her library's social media accounts along with a different single-word theme each week: words that spoke to the social isolation of the times (e.g., "alone") and some that were just fun (e.g., "local," "orange"). Participants submit photos that represent the theme through a form on the library's website, and selected photos are published at the end of the week. "Seeing their photos is such a treat for me as the program facilitator," Strassburg says. "People's visual representations of these themes has been surprising, charming, poignant, and even funny." The library decided to include the photos in a new digital archive, The Preserve Perspective Project.

THREE OREGON POETS

Coos Bay Public Library
Coos Bay, Oregon

Reference librarian Paul Addis had never hosted a virtual poetry event, but he felt it was important to recognize the contributions of artists during the pandemic. "I don't think artists are getting enough credit right now for providing what I think is essential for my sanity," he told a live Zoom audience of 29 people. "All forms of art right now are very important. . . . I've been listening to a lot of music, enjoying a lot of books and poetry, looking at photos and art. That's what keeps me sane." As its name suggests, the program featured readings by three Oregon poets, one of whom had been scheduled to present in person at the library before it closed. The virtual nature of the program did make it difficult to recruit a few poets that Addis originally had in mind, as they didn't want to learn new technology. Still, the audience was larger than similar in-person events have been, Addis said, because it didn't require people to leave home after a day at work. "I had never done a strictly poetry event at my library before but I already have another one scheduled," Addis said. "Sudden demand! Give the patrons what they want!" Two poets who met at the event have since collaborated with other Oregon writers on a book about the art of recent protests, which the library will feature in December.

TO-GO CRAFTS

Liberty Lake Municipal Library
Liberty Lake, Washington

When her library closed to the public, librarian Joanne Percy looked for a way to interact with patrons in a way that wasn't completely online. "When the library is open, I organize craft classes, which are especially popular during the summer months," Percy said. "I decided to continue these classes from home." She created take-home tote bags that contained all the craft materials that adult and teen patrons would need to create six different DIYs, including a decorate your tote bag activity (in which the tote itself was the craft), paper flowers, and clay jewelry bowls and simple bead bracelets. Library staff put the bags together wearing masks and gloves; patrons could request them online or by phone and pick them up curbside. Once at home, the patrons could visit the library's YouTube, Facebook, or Instagram for tutorials for each craft. "It was the closest we could get to our summer in-person programming during this time," Percy said.

VIRTUAL BEER TASTING

Vernon Area Public Library
Lincolnshire, Illinois

Vernon Area Public Library's Virtual Beer Tasting hit several marks: it was educational, supported a local business, and gave more than 80 residents a much-needed beer break. Business outreach librarian Ashley Johnson worked with a local brewmaster to offer the online guided tasting. The library hosted the virtual presentation on Zoom; the brewery provided the program content and a flight of four craft beers, which participants could choose to purchase in advance with curbside delivery. (The $14 library sampler packs sold out.) The presenters tried to livestream through both Zoom and Facebook Live simultaneously, but Zoom turned out to be a better fit because its gallery view allowed participants to see each other, providing an "all-in-the-same-room" feel. "People were chatting to each other in the chat feature, waving to one another, and lifting their glasses to toast at the presenter's request," Johnson said. "The audience became a virtual pub as we toasted each pour together."

VIRTUAL CHECK-INS FOR LIBRARY STAFF

Massachusetts Library System
Marlborough, Massachusetts

The Massachusetts Library System (MLS) is a state-supported collaborative that provides services to 1,600 Massachusetts libraries of all types and sizes. When social distancing shuttered libraries across the Commonwealth in spring 2020, MLS staff heard that staff in the libraries wanted to gather virtually to check in and share ideas about how to serve their communities during that time. In response, MLS consultants held a series of check-ins on library topics, including adult services, teen services, small libraries, and health services. More than 1,600 library staff attended the 35 sessions between March 20 and June 30, most joining from home. "Some of the virtual check-ins drew sizable crowds, so making sure that our virtual platform could accommodate large numbers of participants and provide them with meaningful ways to interact with each other was something we had to work through," said Terry McQuown, MLS consulting and training services director. The gatherings were tried on several platforms, including GoToMeeting, GoToWebinar, GoToTraining, and Zoom; Zoom and GoToMeeting worked best because participants could see each other and use the chat feature.

VIRTUAL COMIC MINI-CON

Bridgeville Public Library and South Fayette Township Library
Bridgeville and Morgan, Pennsylvania

When Bridgeville Public Library and South Fayette Township Library in Pennsylvania partnered to create a virtual comic mini-con, it was all-hands-on-deck. The goal was to create a family-friendly celebration of comic books, movies, graphic novels, anime, comic art, and more, with activities for all ages. Staff started planning the video series in April 2020, shortly after the libraries closed; some of the events were already planned as part of an in-person mini-con, while others were brainstormed for the virtual event. At a virtual meeting, the libraries' programming staff each committed to doing one video or activity. The end result was a series of nine events, released on YouTube, including two videos for children featuring superhero-themed crafts and book recommendations, a session on makeup artistry, DIY demos to create a Pokémon stress ball and paper stars, and a live Dungeons & Dragons panel discussion led by two high school students.

VIRTUAL [SPANISH/FRENCH] CONVERSATION HOUR

Oak Park Public Library
Oak Park, Illinois

Virtual Language Conversation Hours invite already conversant speakers of a second language to practice speaking in a casual setting. Participants strengthen their skills organically while learning about other cultures from their fellow participants. Traditionally, community engagement specialist Nora Sanchez and community engagement librarian Ian Gosse offered their Spanish/French conversation hour at one of their Oak Park Public Library branches just west of Chicago, but the pandemic inspired them to try the program online. The result? Attendance increased from around six to eight regulars to between ten to twelve, including attendees joining from other states and countries. Happily, Oak Park residents found themselves learning a language alongside learners from Connecticut, Maryland, Iran, and Switzerland. "Make it clear at the beginning that all skill levels are welcome and that everyone is here to practice and get to know new people," Sanchez and Gosse advise.

VIRTUAL TALES & TRAVEL

Tempe Public Library
Tempe, Arizona

Retired librarian Mary Beth Riedner created Tales & Travel in 2008 after her husband was diagnosed with young-onset dementia. The experience taught her that, while society tends to stigmatize people with Alzheimer's disease or dementia and focus on the skills that have been lost, "each person with dementia is still a unique individual with their own interests and abilities." Tales & Travel was originally designed as an in-person program model that took people with dementia on a one-hour imaginary trip to another country or area of the United States using library materials. Participants could peruse and read aloud from books carefully selected to capture their interest while maintaining their dignity: travel books and coffee table books with vibrant illustrations, some children's books, and other materials with simple vocabulary and lots of white space. As they browsed, library staff and volunteers engaged the participants in conversation, often chatting about memories sparked by the topics. When COVID-19 shut down many libraries in March 2020, Riedner quickly pivoted and began creating online versions of the program. The series is available as videos or slide presentations and includes locations like Chicago, California, Italy, and Austria. It can be accessed by libraries or individuals at talesandtravelmemories.com/memory-cafes; Riedner plans to add additional trips over the coming months. The virtual version also includes word search puzzles and adult coloring pages that people can do on their own after the program.

WE'RE GONNA MAKE IT!

Cranford Public Library
Cranford, New Jersey

During shelter-in-place, children's librarian Lauren Antolino wanted to host a virtual library program, but she had been sick when her library had closed and hadn't been able to stock up on storytime supplies. "I realized I was probably in the same position as many caregivers, and I started trying to think of activities using materials that most people likely have around the house," she said. What emerged was We're Gonna Make It!, a Friday evening Facebook Live challenge that demonstrated fun and simple crafts using things like cardboard, dish soap, plastic wrap, and aluminum foil, or whatever kids had lying around the house. In quick 2- to 5-minute videos, Antolino makes a cardboard dinosaur, recycled robot, window cling, and more. Participants had the weekend to make their own creations and submit photos of their work by Sunday night to be included in a virtual gallery. And, yes, the name is a play on words: "I really liked the double meaning. My hope was that it would be reassuring to the families who participated," Antolino said.

Five Ways to Be Inclusive in Your Virtual Programs

By nature, virtual programming is not inclusive to everyone because it requires access to technology and the internet. At the same time, virtual programming opens access to people who might not previously have been library users. How can we do our best to create an environment that makes participants feel welcomed and valued? Kristin Lahurd, Amber Hayes, and Gwendolyn Prellwitz from ALA's Office for Diversity, Literacy and Outreach Services (ODLOS) offer some insights:

1. **Set times and conditions that work for the broadest possible audience.** Knowing that your audience will be limited to those with internet access, you should try to make your virtual events convenient in terms of timing and platform. Consider the scheduling needs of parents, caregivers, students, and essential workers—for example, evening programs tend to be better for caretakers and weekends may be better for students—and use platforms that are widely used by your community.
2. **Reflect diversity.** Your presenters should mirror the community you are trying to reach. Approach potential speakers with an eye toward diversity in race, gender, ethnicity, ability, and other identities. This is an opportunity to expand your network and seek out new voices rather than relying on those with whom you usually co-present.
3. **Ask in advance about participants' accessibility needs.** ODLOS staff includes an optional question in the registration pages for their virtual events: "Would you like captioning services for this presentation?" If anyone requests captioning, you can use an automated service or hire a person to do live captioning. Some

videoconferencing platforms also offer captioning services. Be aware, though, that any automated service will be imperfect, and you should expect to clean up the transcript afterward and make it available to participants.

4. **Create ground rules (a.k.a. group agreements).** Group agreements, which are also called ground rules or ground assumptions, set the tone and expectations for the session. They can be a tool for managing conversations; you can refer back to the agreed-upon expectations if the conversation derails or to highlight a particular dynamic.

   Ground rules also demonstrate your intention to create a responsible space. Ground rules can vary depending on the situation. Here are six rules recommended by ODLOS:

   - Be Present. Bring all of yourself to the discussion. Set aside distractions.
   - Everyone is INVITED to speak.
   - Practice self-awareness.
   - Only share what you can carry.
   - Everyone is responsible for this space.
   - Trust people's lived experiences.

5. **Ask for feedback afterwards.** Follow-up surveys are a great way to improve programs. ODLOS asks, "Is there anything that prevented you from engaging during this session?"

NOTE

1. Todd Overman, "A Novel Idea: The Skinny on Fort Worth Public Library's Stay at Home Book Club," *Forth Worth Magazine*, July 23, 2020, https://fwtx.com/culture/a-novel -idea-the-skinny-on-fort-worth-public-library%E2%80%99s-stay-/.

CHAPTER FOUR

ENTERTAINMENT

W e had a lot on our minds in 2020, but let's not downplay the importance of some plain, good-hearted fun. This chapter is for the hot dog costumes, the sidewalk obstacle course, for Mr. Prickles, the hedge-hog cake, and all the other creative programs that brought entertainment to communities. It's also for sliding a chunk of ice down a wet driveway on a hot summer day, because why not?

A MIDSUMMER NIGHT'S STREAM

Russell Library
Middletown, Connecticut

Russell Library collaborated with two local arts organizations—the Oddfel-lows Playhouse Youth Theater and ARTFARM—to put on a four-part Zoom/Facebook Live production of William Shakespeare's *A Midsummer Night's Dream*. Most of the actors were local teens who joined virtually from their homes—some in costume, and with Puck, the mischievous fairy, doing acro-batics on a yoga mat. The play was split up over four evening performances, with local musicians, including the Connecticut State Troubadour, briefly introducing each one. A memorable quote from one of the performances: "Hippolyta, you are muted!" More than 500 people tuned in live over the four evenings, and the Facebook recordings have since amassed thousands of views.

ADULT GAME NIGHT

Cora J. Belden Library
Rocky Hill, Connecticut

Cora J. Belden Library's Adult Game Night is kind of a mash-up between Bingo and *Name That Tune*. Participants listen to 30 to 40 seconds of a song, identify the song title, and mark it off on their Bingo card; word scrambles of the song titles provide an extra clue. The monthly event has been popular, with people even logging in from outside Connecticut to play. "One fan told me she couldn't join the program because the internet in her house wasn't working, so she drove to our library parking lot to access our Wi-Fi and played in her car," says reference librarian Jennifer Zappulla, who also arranges all the music for the events. "She wasn't going to miss it!" In June, the theme was '80s music; in October, contestants showed up in Halloween costumes, and February will be love song themed. Gift cards are distributed to the winners, the players unmute at the end to socialize, and they sing a closing song together. "We frequently get thank you cards from patrons who say it is one of their favorite forms of entertainment now," Zappulla says.

ART NIGHT OUT

Carson City Library
Carson City, Nevada

Art Night Out was a crowd favorite when held in person at Carson City Library, and the same is true now that the program has gone virtual. Jana Wiersma, senior library assistant in the Creative Learning Department, chooses an art project each month that allows patrons to use upcycled materials they may already have at home. Participants log in to Zoom and either watch Wiersma demonstrate the craft or just work on their own craft together with music playing in the background. Creations have included Nevada-shaped coasters made from wine corks, nature portraits made of bits gathered from outdoors, and "imagine your story" dream boards (using the summer library program theme). Patrons share their finished projects with one another and have said they find the gathering relaxing. "This program is all about adults being able to de-stress and just 'be' together," Wiersma says. "The music fills in around my talking and makes it so that no one feels they have to fill in the silence."

BOREDOM BUSTERS!

Pittston Memorial Library
Pittston, Pennsylvania

With kids (and adults) going stir crazy during quarantine, Noelle Kozak started a Facebook Live series with hands-on activities that people could do at home. Activities ranged from ice bowling (you just need balls of ice down a damp driveway) to making a birdfeeder (inspired by her grandmother's love of birdwatching) and throwing a Star Wars party Pizza Party (in honor of May the Fourth). The videos were posted each Thursday afternoon from April through June and attracted up to 500 weekly views. "By offering the program live and also posting the video, we were able to reach so many more people than we would have been able to had we done the program in-house," said Kozak, the library's teen programming coordinator. Doing the videos live was a new experience and an uncomfortable one to start. "I had done videos for the library before, but if I fumbled or made a mistake, I could always go back and re-record. This format really challenged me," she said. "As a result of the pandemic I have grown in learning how to use different forms of technology and feel more comfortable in front of the camera. It has been difficult at times, but the feedback has been amazing."

FAMILY BAKING CHALLENGE

Snake River School/Community Library
Blackfoot, Idaho

Assistant librarian Jennifer Leavitt wanted to encourage families in her farming community to do something together during quarantine. Using the Collaborative Summer Reading Program's 2020 theme of "imagine your story," she decided to host weekly challenges where families would be tasked with baking something related to a theme. When the library read a book about dragons in a weekly virtual storytime, they challenged families to bake or cook food in the shape of a dragon. (One submission was a fire-breathing cake with dry ice in its mouth.) For a superhero theme, one family submitted a "spud cake" in the shape of a potato. They explained that it was an homage to their farming neighbors, who had left potatoes on their doorstep to help them out during this difficult time. "It might seem like a small gesture, but in the eyes of this family, our farmers are the real superheroes in our community," Leavitt says. Participants e-mailed photos of their work to the library, and a weekly winner received a gift card to a local business.

THE GREAT BROOKIE BAKE-OFF

Emmet O'Neal Library
Mountain Brook, Alabama

Emmet O'Neal Library's virtual bake-off was a spin on TV shows like *Nailed It!* and *The Great British Baking Show*. The library had hosted several such competitions in person at the library and they were always a hit, so adult services librarian Amanda Westfall decided to offer an online version. People baked in their own kitchens and everyone was connected over Zoom. Teams did not know the challenge until they logged in, when they were tasked with decorating a cake—two baked and cooled round layer cakes—that looked like a hedgehog using materials that they had on hand in their kitchens (no internet searches allowed). The library paid a go-to craft teacher/professional baker to make a model cake ("Mr. Prickles") and serve as an expert judge. Eleven teams competed—including many families—and there were four judges, including the pro baker, Westfall (who also handled tech) and other library staff. "There was never a lull," Westfall said. Looking back, it was a bad idea to both host the competition and handle the technical aspects of Zoom. "Luckily, one of my coworkers who was there to judge helped me out when I was having technical difficulties." Westfall said she wanted the program to provide a place where people could interact safely during social distancing. "I feel like the teams did get to know each other throughout the night, and one attendee happily said that it is was 'the most people I've seen in a long time!'"

HOT DOG MAN

Carroll County Public Library
New Windsor, Maryland

Librarian Christopher Heady, a.k.a. Mr. Chris, wolfs down ten hot dogs for dinner one night and goes to bed. When he wakes up in the morning, he's alarmed to find that he has mysteriously turned into a hot dog. "Frank! I'm a hot dog!" a hot dog-costumed Mr. Chris screams to his (stuffed) canine sidekick, who tries to take a bite of him. Such begins Carroll County Public Library's hilarious saga of Hot Dog Man. Unable to go outside (he is a hot dog, after all), Mr. Chris visits the library website to research his condition and finds a plethora of fun things to keep him safely occupied at home. Heady started wearing the hot dog costume for storytime in schools and decided to revive the character when the pandemic hit as a way to tell kids and families to hang in there during the quarantine. "It's the kind of message of if this crazy guy can do it, then so can you," Heady told the *Baltimore Sun*. "People are really picking up on it, and I get a lot of messages where people are asking what's happening to Hot Dog Man next."[1] Episodes are available on the library's Facebook page.

IMAGINE YOUR STORY OUTDOOR NO-TOUCH ESCAPE ROOM

McMillan Memorial Library
Wisconsin Rapids, Wisconsin

An escape room—with its close quarters and all those high-touch surfaces—sounds like an ideal breeding ground for the coronavirus, but library assistant Karmen Kelly had a vision. "Our library has had a great deal of success with our escape rooms and have planned to continue adding new ones," Kelly says. "As the pandemic threatened to bring these events to a screeching halt, I knew there had to be a way to build a new escape room and still keep it within the COVID guidelines." The library's newest escape room was built outdoors using sidewalk chalk, disposable game pieces, and an online form, leaving virtually no risk of contamination and freeing library staff from the responsibility of sanitizing items between uses. Designed with the summer reading program theme "imagine your story," the puzzle challenges participants to figure out how their game pieces interact with the drawings in the space to spell out a word. Once they have figured out the answer, they enter it into an online form to see if they got it right. "By using this 'password' method, we've eliminated the need for physical locks," Kelly says. The form contains all the details that players need so staff can stay at a safe distance. There is also a butterfly craft project so players can make use of their disposable game pieces at home.

"I SPY" WINDOWS

Princeton Public Library
Princeton, Wisconsin

Located on the busiest street in their rural Wisconsin town, Princeton Public Library staff wanted to create a safe, outdoor, passive activity that would signal to the community that they were still there during their state's safer-at-home order. They developed an intricate window display based on the classic "I Spy" book series by Jean Marzollo. "We wanted to let our community know that their library is still physically here. These windows serve as a reminder that, even though we have moved many of our services and programming online, the library will continue with many offerings inside of our building when we are safe and ready," says library director Laura Skalitzky. "They also looked great during National Library Week." An instruction sheet taped to the window listed the items that could be found within the display, including eight ladybugs, ten tiny colorful ponies, two crawdads, and a pair of roller skates, while also reminding viewers not to touch the glass.

LAKE OSWEGO PUB(LIC LIBRARY) TRIVIA NIGHT

Lake Oswego Public Library
Lake Oswego, Oregon

It's like pub trivia but shorter—and you're not in a pub. Although snacking and drinking are encouraged! Each Thursday, Lake Oswego Public Library puts on its "pub" hat to host an evening trivia game. The program is hosted by two librarians, one of whom writes the questions each week. The game consists of 30 questions in six rounds—including a visual ID round (with themes like national parks or muscle cars) and a *Name That Tune* round—and they use TriviaMaker software to make it look like a *Jeopardy!* board. Patrons work in teams from their homes to submit answers via a Google Form. The hosts score the answers, announce standings every two rounds, and the winner gets an e-card to Powell's Books. The response was enthusiastic—so much so that they had to recruit an additional librarian to help add up the scores between rounds. "It's really fun for the hosts and the contestants," says reference librarian Chris Myers. The librarians recommend that players sign in from home using two devices: one to see and hear the questions and one to submit their answers via a Google Form. The teams can be as large as people want to make them, and teammates do not need to be in the same location, making it extra quarantine friendly; one team has eight members scattered across the country.

LEGO BUILDING CHALLENGE

Santa Cruz Public Libraries
Aptos, California

Librarian Sandi Imperio has hosted LEGO Simple Machines and robotics programs at her library for the past eight years, but for a quarantine-friendly online version, she wanted something that could reach a larger base. "I wanted to create a program that only used common LEGO pieces for those who don't have the more expensive specialty pieces or motors," Imperio said. "I also wanted to avoid doing a live demonstration to be more inclusive for those with limited internet access." Throughout summer reading, she e-mailed a basic building challenge and an intermediate level "bonus build" to a list of registered participants. (One example: build a freestanding structure that is at least ten inches tall and five times bigger at the top than at the bottom.) Photos of the completed builds could be posted to a closed Facebook group created by the library. If members didn't have a Facebook account and didn't want to create one, they were asked to e-mail the photos to Imperio so she could post for them, or to just share with family and friends.

OPEN MIC ONLINE

Katonah Village Library
Katonah, New York

Katonah Village Library decided to make their social media channels a show-case for community talent during COVID-19. Any form of self-expression is accepted: "Video yourself playing/singing/acting/reciting/dancing/slamming/joking/monologuing/miming/what have you, then send us a link," the library's event listing requests. Library staff adds a selection of videos to the library's YouTube channel, then shares an e-blast of the week's submissions each

Saturday to a list of folks who opt in. One video per week is highlighted on the library's Facebook page. The submissions have included a middle school student playing the ukulele and singing Bruno Mars's "You Can Count on Me," a dedication to her best friend who had to have her bat mitzvah celebration in isolation during quarantine, and a third grader singing the original song "What About That?" about all the things she missed during quarantine. The series has overall been a success, says engagement and special projects librarian Michael Robin, but he mentions a couple cautions: "Uneven submission rates mean feast-or-famine for weeks; there is no way to know in advance what it would be. Also, curation can hurt feelings: for example, a proud parent's masterpiece might be someone else's crashing bore, or a well-intentioned COVID-19 joke might be taken as stunningly offensive."

PAINTING WITH BOB ROSS

Abington Community Library
Clarks Summit, Pennsylvania

Bob Ross, the late American painter and famed host of *The Joy of Painting*, has a voice so soothing that it could fix just about anything. During the chaos of the early pandemic days, the Abington Community Library's teen leadership committee created Painting with Bob Ross. The concept was simple: the teens met on Zoom and followed along with a Bob Ross painting video on Netflix while drawing and painting together. Eight teens showed up, and "it was lovely to see the creativity and initiative of our teen volunteers," said head of youth services Laura Gardoski.

READ TO SHELDON

Brandywine Community Library
Topton, Pennsylvania

When Brandywine Community Library was offering services in-person, Sheldon's favorite thing to do was sit and listen to stories. The 33-year-old Greek tortoise is a favorite buddy of summer readers, who can join the Sheldon Club by reading him a book at least once every six weeks. When COVID-19 shut the library doors, staff came up with a workaround. "Sheldon misses all his friends reading to him at the library," the library announced. "Now we have a solution!" About 12 kids per week signed up via a Google Form to read to Sheldon for 15 minutes, and a staff member helped the tortoise connect via Zoom. "The kids loved seeing him on the screen and he sat, for the most part, and listened to them read," said library director Heather Wicke. An unexpected bonus of reading to Sheldon from home: siblings jumped on the bandwagon when they saw their brother or sister reading to him and wanted to do it too. "It was a great way to see faces and talk to the children while we were not able to gather together," Wicke said.

RETRO AEROBICS ONLINE

La Grange Park Public Library
La Grange Park, Illinois

Retro Aerobics Online is a low-impact exercise program for adults that follows a different vintage workout routine each month, such as Richard Simmons's *Sweatin' to the Oldies*. Inspired by the success of a library Zumba program, children's services and reference assistant Christina McPhail created the program for in-person meetings but transitioned online during the pandemic. Setup was easy. "I simply start the Zoom meeting five minutes before the program was scheduled to begin to make sure everything was working smoothly and to have the workout video ready to go. Once my attendees had joined the meeting, we chatted for a minute," McPhail says. "Once everyone was ready, I shared my screen of the workout video and we all followed and laughed along." McPhail recommends choosing a low-intensity, low-impact workout for at least the first meeting to ensure that it is safe for all involved. She also gave a safety disclaimer at the beginning of the class and periodically reminded everyone to drink water.

SILLY SIDEWALK OBSTACLE COURSE

Tavares Public Library
Tavares, Florida

During summer 2020, patrons of all ages started making trips to the Tavares Public Library for something besides curbside pickup. In an attempt to bring some fun and levity to an otherwise serious time, reference librarian Marli Lopez designed a 126-foot, self-directed obstacle course—consisting of bunny hops, singing, and skipping—on the sidewalk outside the library. "The Silly Sidewalk Obstacle Course offers a sense of liberation and fun while emphasizing the importance of wellness during these unprecedented COVID-19 times," says library director Rebecca Campbell. The course was laid out using duct tape rather than sidewalk chalk to withstand the Florida summer rain—and it has withstood it so well that, with a few "face-lifts," the course was still up and running in November. "The duct tape has survived both the weather and the wear and tear of many happy feet," Campbell says. "It's bringing much happiness to our little town."

SONGS FROM THE STACKS

Nederland Community Library
Nederland, Colorado

After patrons go home, Nederland Community Library turns into a recording space for an ongoing virtual concert series in the style of NPR's *Tiny Desk*. The library invites local musicians and bands to perform three to five original songs using world-class video and audio equipment. "As Nederland has always been a hub for live music, we began this project as a service to our patrons—as a way to keep live music alive in the midst of a global shutdown," says library assistant Charlie Westerink. "We didn't initially think of this as a service to the musicians, but it has turned out to be extremely valuable to them as well, and I now receive a number of inquiries each week from musicians interested in performing for the series." The musicians can use the high-quality recordings to develop their electronic press kit, and the library posts the videos as individual tracks on Facebook, where they have received thousands of views.

The Strategy of Being Yourself, Even—Especially—if You Are a Weirdo

Nederland, Colorado, a town of about 1,500 in the foothills of Boulder, is . . . quirky. Need proof? Look no further than Frozen Dead Guy Days, an annual celebration honoring the late Bredo Morstoel, a.k.a. Grandpa, who since 1989 has been cryogenically frozen in a shed near town.

Nederland Community Library is well-loved and has become even more so during the pandemic. In the interview that follows, library assistant Charlie Westerink discusses how he creates content that is both true to the library's character and strategic, and how doing so has increased video viewership by an amazing 3,400 percent in 28 days.

Your social media engagement has gone through the roof during COVID-19. What do you attribute that success to?

When Colorado went into stay-at-home orders in March, we were one of the few libraries in the state that remained open. During this time, a coworker and I started dressing up in costumes and formalwear. We quickly realized that these social media posts were extremely popular. As we expanded our virtual programming, we kept this in mind and worked to showcase our quirky sense of humor, and all the things that make Ned weird and great.

Our goal with our social media posts is to present the library as fun, quirky, approachable, and human, but also as a reliable and unbiased source of information during a time when misinformation has run wild. It's all about relationship building. As an example, we posted a storytime video a few weeks ago in which Mr. Mike mentioned several times that he was hungry. The video went live at 10 a.m., and by 10:45 a concerned patron had dropped off a brown-bag lunch with an apple and a peanut butter and jelly sandwich "for the hungry librarian."

That sounds fun, but I suspect there is also some strategy behind your success!

We work hard to establish quantifiable goals and put out content that is on-brand, geared toward patrons' interests, and produced to the highest quality standards. For example, The Streaming (a one-minute, Halloween-themed video) was designed to promote awareness and attract new subscribers. It lands squarely at the wide top of the video marketing funnel. In contrast, storytime is a service we provide to remain connected with our existing patrons—it falls at the narrower end of the funnel.

How often do you post new videos?

We have experimented with various release schedules for video content and social media posts. At one point, we were putting out three to four videos per week. As our videos become more elaborate, we've reduced to two to three videos. We release storytime on Fridays and Songs from the Stacks on Wednesdays or Saturdays. We've found that concise videos do better than lengthier ones, so storytimes have gone from 20–30 minutes to about five. We see much more consistent viewership with this format. We modeled Songs from the Stacks as single song releases partly for this reason.

All of this must take a lot of time.

Yes. Planning and preparation pay MASSIVE dividends. Our most popular videos would not have been possible without detailed shooting scripts and shot lists, and our book trailers are only possible thanks to a variety of checklists and templates that we create prior to shooting.

What would you say is the most important aspect of a successful video?

Technically speaking, sound. Viewers are much more likely to forgive poor video quality than poor sound. Very respectable videos can be made with a smartphone, especially with some consideration of proper lighting; however, a good-quality microphone is absolutely critical. It pays to listen to the sound while you're recording. We've lost a few due to mic handling noise and other surprises.

In terms of strategy, I would say it is knowing your audience. We recently moved from YouTube as our primary method of distribution to Facebook. It has demonstrated the importance of delivering content to your audience on the correct platform. It may seem intimidating to start a virtual program from scratch, but if a bunch of simple mountain librarians can do it, anyone can!

Do you have any parting words for us?

The face of libraries is changing, whether we like it or not. One surefire way to humanize libraries and set them apart from the faceless, mirthless internet is to celebrate and showcase their personalities. We're still here, we're serious about what we do, and we know how to laugh about it! As with all things in life, if it's worth doing it's worth overdoing. Right?

SUMMER TWEEN: HAPPILY NEVER AFTER

Vestavia Hills Library in the Forest
Vestavia Hills, Alabama

Jack (of beanstalk fame), Robin Hood, Belle, and Gretel are called into the police station for questioning. The four characters had been at Little Red Riding Hood's book club the night before and were now suspects in the investigation of the theft of a rare ruby stolen from Red's house. Who committed the crime? Staff at Vestavia Hills Library in the Forest recorded the whodunnit video, lacing it with clues; every time one of the characters mentioned an item found on the scene, tweens were asked to mark it off on their investigative worksheet, which tweens could download and print. The character with the most checks at the end was the thief. Filming took place at the library, which was closed to the public at the time. "It was so much fun and made everyone who watched it laugh," said library assistant Holly Parker, who wrote the script. "Going virtual with programs has really opened me up to a new world." The video was posted to the library's YouTube channel and also posted to Facebook and the library's website.

TOTAL REQUEST LIVE: BPL PIANO SHOW! FEATURING KALEEN DOLAN

Bloomingdale Public Library
Bloomingdale, Illinois

Bloomingdale Public Library was looking for interactive, virtual programs that were different from the typical online lectures and webinars. They came up with BPL Piano Show, an all-request piano performance streamed on Facebook Live. Since May 2020, the show has featured Kaleen Dolan, a born-and-raised Chicagoan and professional pianist who has played at top piano bars across the country and world. Each week, Dolan takes requests for an hourlong show, from Rod Stewart to Lady Gaga to Natalie Imbruglia; some hours have been on themes, such as British Invasion or Disney. "The program has increased community engagement, cultural enrichment through musical programs, support of a local artist, and increased interaction on our social media pages," says Jessica Frazier, assistant department head of adult services. The show has seen repeat attendees and it is common to see dozens of requests during the show. The cost to the library is $75 to $100 per show; Dolan also accepts tips via her Venmo account. While originally the show was only scheduled through August 2020, it has been extended and remains popular. "When this COVID is under control we want to see you at the piano bar!" commented one viewer in October.

VIRTUAL LITERARY LEGOS

Seneca Falls Library
Seneca Falls, New York

Have you ever wanted to recreate a work of literature in LEGOs? Kids in Seneca Falls, New York, can—and without even leaving their homes. Virtual Literacy LEGOs is a virtual children's program offered in three parts: (1) a Zoom session in which youth services coordinator Tara Montoney reads a surprise (unadvertised) story, asking the kids to pay particular attention to the visuals and think about something they could create with LEGOs; (2) a 90-minute break, when everyone logs off and works on their LEGO creations at home for as long as they want; and (3) a second show-and-tell Zoom session where Montoney calls on each child to show and describe their creation. If participants don't have LEGOs, they can use clay, blocks, Play-Doh, or any other medium they like. Afterward, everyone is encouraged to take a photo of their masterpiece and post it on the library's Facebook page. "This program is so adaptable, in fact, that I'm going to try a session just for adults!" Montoney says. "It doesn't take much time to run, but the reward is huge."

VIRTUAL MINECRAFT CLUB

Silver City Public Library
Silver City, New Mexico

Silver City Public Library offered an in-person Minecraft Club. When COVID hit, the library's young adult librarian created an online adaptation of the club for kids ages six and up to collaborate and compete with other local Minecraft plans. The library made its own private Minecraft Realm, which allows up to ten players to play together at any time, even when the weekly one-hour library program ends. The library must invite players to its Realm, which helps with security, and kids must have an internet connection, a supported device, and the Minecraft game software. When it comes to playtime, a librarian plays alongside the kids, chats in the chat box, and surveys what participants have built in the Realm. A word of caution: if your library doesn't already have a Minecraft Realms subscription, make sure you purchase the correct version for the devices that your participants will be using. "Generally speaking, Minecraft for Java is the 'original' version of the game, most likely to be used by people playing Minecraft on a Mac desktop/laptop computer or a Windows 7 or older computer," says MJ Medel, formerly Silver City Public Library's children's and young adult librarian. "We chose the newer Minecraft and Minecraft Realms Plus because it works on the library Nintendo Switch, the library Xbox, and on the devices that a majority of our community members are using."

VIRTUAL NATURE WALK

Grove Family Library
Chambersburg, Pennsylvania

"This is Grove Family Library coming to you this morning from Cowans Gap State Park," begins a simple 50-second video clip posted to the library's Facebook page on March 27. Such began the library's Virtual Nature Walk series. The videos evolved from a monthly library program; when the pandemic hit, the library began posting short snippets of state parks and nature hikes to social media each week. The posts became a virtual space for residents to share memories and feelings about the locations while people were social distancing. It also offered a way for the library to stay in touch with its community. "We do this as a reminder of how important it is for you to get out and about each and every day in the fresh air and sunshine if at all possible," staff said in the first video. "We're looking forward to the day the library is reopened again, and until such time we say to you, be healthy our friends."

VIRTUAL SCARY STORIES

Aram Public Library
Delavan, Wisconsin

Katherine Schoofs, youth services librarian and assistant director, and Linnea Bergstrom, library assistant, at Aram Public Library were looking for a way to connect with teens and tweens during Wisconsin's stay-at-home order when they came up with the idea for Virtual Scary Stories. The idea was simple enough: record and edit scary stories—or at least really, really eerie ones—at home. Schoofs and her husband figured out a spooky set, lighting, and camera angles, while Bergstrom created opening credits with glimpses of a cloudy night sky and a "Devil" tarot card. For showtime, Schoofs gives the "all quiet on set" call to her seven-year-old and three dogs and does a short reading, anywhere from three to ten minutes. The videos are pushed out on the library's Instagram and YouTube accounts on Saturday nights. "Don't be afraid to utilize what you have on hand, whether it be location, costuming, or what-have-you," advises library director Michelle Carter. "And don't be afraid to show off your inner creepy and BE OK with looking/feeling silly! If you're having fun and embracing the eerie vibe, your patrons will buy in."

VIRTUAL STAR WARS FAN FILM FESTIVAL

Piscataway Public Library
Piscataway, New Jersey

Did the world break a record on May 4 for the number of Darth Vaders simulaneously logged onto the internet? Chances are good. Perhaps a handful came from Piscataway, New Jersey, where the public library hosted a two-hour mini-marathon of *Star Wars* films, trivia, and costume contests in honor of May the Fourth Be with You Day. Using Zoom, participants viewed fan films that were available on YouTube, including "Hoshino" and "Dark Jedi." "We had really great conversations about the fan films, and the viewings went better than we expected," said Westgard branch manager/teen services librarian Erica Krivopal. "We had concerns about how the films would display while screen sharing, but everything ran smoothly." Participants played two rounds of trivia and finally had a show-and-tell where participants could show off their most beloved collectibles and crafts.

Leading a Virtual Film Discussion in Seven Steps

Nearly as ubiquitous to libraries as book clubs, films are great conversation starters, even when you can't meet in person. Here Juan Rubio, program manager for digital media and learning at the Seattle Public Library, shares his seven steps to a successful discussion:

1. **Prepare.** Get familiar with the film. Watch it in advance and identify themes for your discussion. Ideally, the conversation will flow naturally, but you should still have a list of questions to guide you. Also consider tech: allow plenty of time prior to the scheduled discussion and make sure your platform is working and everyone knows how to use it. For film discussions, the online platform Discord is a good fit; other options include Zoom, Google Meet, Netflix Party, or Slack.

   You will also need to consider whether to do the film screening itself synchronously or asynchronously. Asking people to watch a film on their own time before the discussion is one way to format a program; this allows you to spend your time together talking.

   While it's a bit trickier logistically, you could host a live viewing party. Netflix Party is one platform for this, although participants need their own Netflix accounts and interactions are limited to a chat box. YouTube Premiere lets you view content available on YouTube. You can also screen films using Zoom or other video platforms by sharing your sound (under Advanced Settings in Zoom)—but make sure you have the proper public screening permissions before you do.

2. **Do an icebreaker.** Once your participants are logged in and you've gone over the relevant tech items, do an icebreaker, such as "What film would you take with you to a desert island?" If you have a large group, get responses from a few volunteers and move on.

3. **Ask who has watched the film.** Do an informal poll to see how many people have watched the film already. Ask them to type a yes or no into the chat or give a thumbs-up on the screen.

4. **Ask for a recap.** Begin by asking a volunteer to summarize the film in two or three minutes. If this seems daunting, offer a famously succinct example: "Dorothy takes flight during a tornado with her dog, Toto, and enters a magical world. She learns about human characteristics such as courage, intelligence, and love. She battles evil and later discovers that it was all an illusion."

5. **Start the discussion.** Begin with general questions such as: What stood out to you in the film? Is there anything that surprised you? Did you learn anything new by watching the film? If so, what was it?

6. **Ask more specific questions.** What was the film's message? Was there more than one message? What creative choices did the filmmaker use to deliver the message?

7. **Conclude.** Sometimes this is as simple as thanking everyone for coming or inviting everyone to unmute for some social time. If you viewed a documentary or a film related to current events, this is a great opportunity to talk about moving to action. Ask: is there anything you might do or say differently as a result of viewing this film? Are there any specific actions you're planning to implement? Present a list of organizations doing work in your area where the participants can learn more, get involved, or advocate with elected officials.

NOTE

1. Megan Woodward, "'Hot Dog Man,' Broadcasting to Your Living Room: Carroll County Library Employee's Videos Entertaining Kids," *Baltimore Sun*, August 5, 2020, https://www.baltimoresun.com/maryland/carroll/news/cc-carroll-library-hot-dog -man-20200805-c6scipcfxvexjhlnvupejqtk3i-story.html.

RESOURCES

PROGRAMMINGLIBRARIAN.ORG

ProgrammingLibrarian.org, the website run by ALA's Public Programs Office, provides resources, connections, and opportunities to help libraries fill their role as centers of lifelong learning. It is a place for library professionals to share, learn, and be inspired to present excellent programming for their communities. Through resources, ideas, and professional development opportunities, we seek to help libraries fill their role as cultural and civic hubs in their communities. Sign up for the Programming Librarian e-newsletter at programminglibrarian.org/newsletter.

PROGRAMMING LIBRARIAN INTEREST GROUP

The Programming Librarian Interest Group (PLIG) is an ALA member initiative group. The group's mission is to bring together all types of librarians interested in public programming for their patrons. Connect with members via the Programming Librarian Facebook Group at www.facebook.com/groups/ProgrammingLibrarianInterestGroup.

LIBRARIES TRANSFORMING COMMUNITIES

Since 2014, ALA's community engagement initiative Libraries Transforming Communities has reimagined the role libraries play in supporting communities. Libraries of all types have utilized free dialogue and deliberation training and resources to lead community and campus forums; take part in anti-violence activities; provide a space for residents to come together and discuss challenging topics; and have productive conversations with civic leaders, library trustees, and staff. Learn more at ala.org/LTC.

ALA PUBLIC PROGRAMS OFFICE

The ALA Public Programs Office empowers libraries to create vibrant hubs of learning, conversation, and connection in communities of all types. Our staff works closely with librarians, humanities scholars, artists and documentarians, STEM and financial literacy experts, and others to create nationwide programming opportunities, grants, and traveling exhibitions for U.S. libraries. Learn more at www.ala.org/ppo or learn about current grant opportunities at www.ala.org/apply.

OTHER ALA EDITIONS BOOKS FROM THE ALA PUBLIC PROGRAMS OFFICE

Ask, Listen, Empower: Grounding Your Library Work in Community Engagement edited by Mary Davis Fournier and Sarah Ostman, 2020, https://www.alastore.ala.org/content/ask-listen-empower-grounding-your-library-work-community-engagement.

Book Club Reboot: 71 Creative Twists by Sarah Ostman and Stephanie Saba, 2019, www.alastore.ala.org/content/book-club-reboot-71-creative-twists.

Rainy Day Ready: Financial Literacy Programs and Tools edited by Melanie Welch and Patrick Hogan, 2020, www.alastore.ala.org/content/rainy-day-ready-financial-literacy-programs-and-tools.

INDEX

CPSIA information can be obtained
at www.ICGtesting.com
Printed in the USA
LVHW031256300921
698968LV00006B/12